Situating Islam

Religion in Culture: Studies in Social Contest and Construction

Series Editor: Russell T. McCutcheon, University of Alabama

This series is based on the assumption that those practices we commonly call religious are social practices that are inextricably embedded in various contingent, cultural worlds. Authors in this series therefore do not see the practices of religion occupying a socially or politically autonomous zone, as is the case for those who use 'and' as the connector between 'religion' and 'culture'. Rather, the range of human performances that the category 'religion' identifies can be demystified by translating them into fundamentally social terms; they should therefore be seen as ways of waging the ongoing contest between groups vying for influence and dominance in intra- and inter-cultural arenas. Although not limited to one historical period, cultural site, or methodological approach, each volume exemplifies the tactical contribution to be made to the human sciences by writers who refuse to study religion as irreducibly religious; instead, each author conceptualizes religion – as well as the history of scholarship on religion – as among the various *arts de faire*, or practices of everyday life, upon which human communities routinely draw when defining and reproducing themselves in opposition to others.

Published titles in the series:

Religion and the Domestication of Dissent:
Or, How to Live in a Less than Perfect Nation
Russell T. McCutcheon

The Symbolic Jesus: Historical Scholarship, Judaism and
the Construction of Contemporary Identity
William E. Arnal

Representing Religion:
Essays in History, Theory and Crisis
Tim Murphy

Forthcoming:

It's Just Another Story: The Politics of Remembering the Earliest Christians
Willi Braun

In Search of Origins: An Introduction to a Theory of Religion
Gary Lease

Japanese Mythology: Hermeneutics on Scripture
Jun'Ichi Isomae

Situating Islam

The Past and Future of an Academic Discipline

Aaron W. Hughes

equinox

LONDON   OAKVILLE

Published by Equinox Publishing Ltd.
UK: Unit 6, The Village, 101 Amies St., London SW11 2JW
USA: DBBC, 28 Main Street, Oakville, CT 06779

www.equinoxpub.com

First published 2007

© Aaron W. Hughes 2007

All rights reserved. No part of this publication may be reproduced or transmitted in any form or by any means, electronic or mechanical, including photocopying, recording or any information storage or retrieval system, without prior permission in writing from the publishers.

British Library Cataloguing-in-Publication Data

ISBN   978 1 84553 259 8   (hardback)
ISBN   978 1 84553 260 4   (paperback)

A catalogue record for this book is available from the British Library.

Library of Congress Cataloging-in-Publication Data

Hughes, Aaron W.
  Situating Islam : the past and future of an academic discipline/Aaron W. Hughes
     p. cm. — (Religion in culture)
  Includes bibliographical references and index.
   ISBN 13: 978-1-84553-259-8 (hb) — ISBN 978-1-84553-260-4 (pb) 1. Islam—Study and teaching. 2. Islam—Research. I. Title. II. Series.
  BP42.H84 2008
  297.071—dc22
                    2007019391

Typeset by S.J.I. Services, New Delhi
Printed and bound in Great Britain by Lightning Source UK Ltd, Milton Keynes, and Lightning Source Inc., La Vergne, TN

J. Samuel Preus
(1933–1998)
in memoriam

The naturalistic approach [to religion]...takes theological interpretations seriously as part of the religious data but not of their explanation; for, as Occam held, explanatory entities (such as "transcendence" or innate religious instincts) must not be multiplied beyond necessity. The naturalistic approach is at once more modest and more ambitious than the religious one: more modest because it is content to investigate the causes, motivations, meanings, and impact of religious phenomena without pronouncing on their cosmic significance for human destiny; ambitious, in that the study of religion strives to explain religion and to integrate its understanding into the other elements of culture to which it is related (Preus 1987, 211).

j.m.h.
ad vitam

Contents

Acknowledgements	ix
Introduction	1
Chapter 1 Loss of Memory, Loss of Focus: Geiger, Said, and the Search for Missing Origins	9
Chapter 2 The Invention of the Middle East: Religion and the Quest for Understanding the Muslim Mind	33
Chapter 3 Tensions Past, Tensions Future: Middle Eastern Studies Confronts Religious Studies	49
Chapter 4 We Study Muslim Constructions, Not Muslims, Right?	72
Chapter 5 The Implosion of a Discipline: 9/11 and the Islamic Studies Scholar as Media Expert	93
Conclusion: Towards a Future Imperfect	112
Notes	117
Bibliography	121
Subject Index	128
Index of Names	131

Acknowledgements

Research for this book was made possible by the generosity of the Social Sciences and Humanities Research Council of Canada (SSHRC), which provided me with a Standard Research Grant for the years 2004–2007. I am also grateful to the Lady Davis Fellowship Trust at the Hebrew University of Jerusalem for awarding me a Lady Davis professorship during the 2005–2006 academic year. The Killam Residential Fellowship Trust at the University of Calgary provided me with a semester leave to finish the writing of this project.

I would especially like to acknowledge Russell McCutcheon who several times encouraged me to write this book at moments when I was increasingly frustrated with the regnant discourse in Islamic studies. I am pleased that this will appear in his series at Equinox. I would also like to thank Janet Joyce, the director of the press, and Sarah Norman, who copyedited the manuscript. Others with whom I have discussed this project include Bill Arnal, Willi Braun, Jennifer Hall, Lisa Hughes, Darlene Juschka, Francis Landy, Steven Wasserstrom, and Elliot Wolfson. I dedicate this book, in part, to Sam Preus, who first taught me the importance of approaching religion naturalistically; and, in part, to j.m.h. who continues to teach me that there is more.

Other important influences on my thinking about theory and method more generally include Robert Ford Campany, David Haberman, and Robert Orsi. All mistakes that remain are solely my own.

Introduction

> This is a book written by infidels for infidels, and it is based on what from any Muslim perspective must appear an inordinate testimony of infidel sources. Our account is not merely unacceptable; it is also one which any Muslim whose faith is as a grain of mustard seed should find no difficulty in rejecting (Crone and Cook 1977, viii).

What follows, and here I take my cue from Crone and Cook's caveat, is quite unabashedly a book written by an infidel, both religiously and academically, for those that I hope will be convinced of the merits of infidelity. My premise, initially stated in the baldest and most general terms, is that the regnant discourses both developed and borrowed by the academic study of Islam have largely proven to be ineffective and outmoded when it comes to explaining Islamic data. Although the academic study of Islam, in the aftermath of 9/11, is currently one of the most sought-after areas of expertise in universities and colleges throughout North America, the failure of nerve on the part of Islamicists to engage seriously reductionist and social-scientific approaches to the study of religion, their unwillingness to move beyond the safety of understanding to the messiness of explanation, has brought us to a critical crossroads. I submit that either this academic discipline can bury its head in the sand of essentialism (e.g., "Islam is x," "Islam is not-x") or it can move beyond such confessionalism in favor of a much more rigorous, self-reflexive set of theoretical questions.

This study attempts both to trace the genealogical trajectories that have brought us from there to here, and to begin the process of suggesting a new set of theoretical prisms when it comes to refracting Islamic data. My main focus, and this demands immediate clarity, will be on the various modes and modalities within the study of Islam that have emerged out of a discipline, itself highly contested and problematic, known as "religious studies."[1] Less concerned with area studies programs such as Near Eastern studies or Middle Eastern studies, I have instead chosen to examine the various contortions, strategies, and coping mechanisms used to bring the study of Islam under the rather flimsy canopy that the so-called academic study of religion supports. As I shall demonstrate below this was not an innocent or coincidental change in orientation; rather it represented a conscious attempt by several important scholars at key historical moments to adopt and adapt a model of religion that stressed faith over cultural production, interiority over external forms, and spirituality over socio-rhetorical legitimation.)

What follows documents – historically, ideologically, and politically – the origins, fluctuations, current malaise, and future prospects of something that is referred to by both its practitioners and critics as "the study of Islam." Theoretically my critical musings and intellectual moorings, as will be evident shortly, emanate from the critical discourses of certain voices within religious studies that regard "religion" as nothing more or less than a byproduct (one of many) of human socio-cognitive activity.

If it is not already clear by implication then let me state simply that this monograph is not about Islam, but about presenting a theoretical study that seeks to uncover how and why practitioners of an academic discipline imagine and construct what they do. The formation of Islamic studies as a scholarly discourse, I contend, is contingent upon the creation of a vocabulary and a set of categories responsible for manufacturing the data that it deems significant or not. The discovery of raw data, the manufacturing of theoretical or hermeneutical frameworks that make sense of such data, and subsequent scholarly conventions responsible for its dissemination are always mediated by particular social, ideological, and political contexts. This book will document these contexts in the creation of the discipline known as Islamic studies and demonstrate how such contexts have been instrumental in shaping how we think about Islam in both the academy and, especially post 9/11, in the media. *Situating Islam* will argue that knowledge of Islam has never been innocent or about the simple collection of facts, but that the interpretive lenses used to study Islam have always been and continue to be caught up with larger forces (e.g., the reform of Judaism, Orientalism, identity politics of the 1960s, 9/11, the fight against terrorism, the creation of a liberal Islam).

One of the main questions in which I am interested, yet surprisingly one that is rarely asked, is what happens when we read the scholarly literature produced on Islam not as secondary literature, but instead as primary data? That is, how and why do scholars of Islam construct theories the way they do, and how do these theories, in turn, predetermine what type of Islam will be found? Making sense of individuals, whether in another period or in contemporary times, let alone something referred to as an entire religious tradition or civilization, is quite simply impossible. The very creation and dissemination of a monolithic entity such as religion or Islam all too often implies a uniformity – be it historical, intellectual, ontological or geographical – that neither can nor does exist in reality. Yet all too often we are willing to assume that such an entity does indeed exist and from which point we then proceed to develop a hermeneutic or series of hermeneutics that we assume further brings this entity to light. Despite such conceptual and logical difficulties, many nonetheless persist in the endeavor to create, through an elaborate system of presences and absences, an "Islam" amenable to or distinct from the aims of something equally slippery, ill-defined, and that more often than not goes by the name of "modernity." Worthwhile here are the comments of Robert A. Orsi, who argues that the academic study of religion, especially in America, has always been intimately connected to the formation of a "true religion," one that was imagined to fit nicely with mainstream American liberal values (2005, 186). In the following statement, for example, Orsi suggests that various forms of Christian alterities, perceived as barbarians at the gates, have always threatened the contours or parameters of such an elitely constructed "true" religion:

> Proponents of the academic study of religion claimed a place in university culture by claiming that the study of "religion" – meaning the denominationally neutral version of Christianity recast as an ethical system – was good and even necessary for American democracy. Outside the walls of the academy, the winds of religious "madness" howled (in the view of those inside) – fire-baptized people, ghost dancers, frenzied preachers and gullible masses, Mormons and Roman Catholics. "Religion" as it took shape in the academy was explicitly imagined in relation to these others and as a prophylactic against them (2005, 186).

It is suggestive to replace "Christianity" or "religion" here with "Islam." Indeed, I take Orsi's words as my point of departure and submit in the pages that follow that we all too frequently witness the construction of a noumenal Islam by scholars who should know better, but who still continue with such attempts for a variety of political and apologetical reasons. Nowhere is this more palpable than in the aftermath of the attacks of September 11, 2001, where many scholars of Islam were all too quick to bracket off something that often coincided remarkably with so-called "Western" values and to which they subsequently attached labels such as "authentic" or "real." All that could not be neatly subsumed under this veritable (and constructed) religious tradition was then circumscribed using labels like "terrorist," "illegitimate," or "fringe."

In many ways, this book had its genesis in my discomfort with precisely these kinds of essentialist constructions. Rather than take such categories as axiomatic or self-evident, I instead decided to track, trace, and ultimately unravel some of the tangled genealogical threads that have gone into such constructions. Instead of beginning with the premise that there exists something called "Islam," often a trope used to preserve something from the pernicious influences of ambivalence and ambiguity,

I here argue that "Islam" is in many ways a construction that emerges out of a series of discourses manufactured in the western academy. This is certainly not to claim that Muslims do not exist, but that a world religion referred to collectively as "Islam" is not itself an innocent term that reflects a specific mode of being in the world, but is something that emerges at a particular historical moment in Europe's thinking about itself (Masuzawa 2005, 186–92). My interest is not so much that scholars of Islam have used and continue to employ such essentialist terms and categories, but where these terms and categories came from. Why did they enter the discipline when they did? What forces, both intellectual and extra-intellectual, were and are responsible for their staying power? What sort of external forces led to the imaginings of and fascinations with such an essentialist construction, an "Islam" that neither could nor would admit of variations?

Moving briefly from the plane of theory to that of praxis, I suggest that the multiple cultural, political, culinary, and artistic processes in which Islam has historically been embedded make it virtually impossible to extricate something that we often have no qualms about extricating and labeling as "Islam," "Islamic civilization," or the "religion of Islam." On the contrary, I suggest that it is precisely by such acts of extrication that we have invented "Islam," by making "Islamic data" emerge from philological, philosophical, mystical, and theological systems that can be accessed in and through texts (the older the better) and divorced from bodies. (Here I follow the comments in J. Z. Smith 1982, xi–xii.) Despite our protestations to the contrary, we differ little from our nineteenth-century predecessors.

This and other genealogies, as I hope to show, are not disinterested, nor are they devoid of manifold political and ideological concerns or desires, all of which seek to grid the strange, the exotic, the unwieldy into safe and discrete categories. A theme that weaves throughout all of the chapters that follow is that unless a discipline takes its genealogies seriously, it risks repeating slogans as if they were axioms that accurately explain the natural order. Such repetition, however, will inevitably lead to the ossification and ultimate collapse of the discipline we now know or recognize as Islamic studies.

Only such a reorientation will help clear the conceptual ground of what it means to study Islam, thus paving the way for new theoretical and hopefully practical architectures. I am particularly critical, as should now be readily apparent, of an essentializing discourse that desires to create an Islam of the spirit, that upholds this Islam as authentic, and to which rival Islams are subsequently evaluated. My goal, stated more theoretically, is to develop a metadiscourse on a particular set of traditions that are often

Introduction

referred to by the name "Islam" by a scholarly community that tends not to engage in the discretely philosophical discourse of the type that I try to engage in here. Let me be clear and state that even though I am often critical of what passes for regnant discourses in the study of Islam, I certainly do not want to imply that the discipline in which this study often finds itself, religious studies, is somehow more comfortable with or self-reflexive of its first principles. On the contrary, this latter discipline is often as problematically configured as Islamic studies, if not more so.

Theories of the Other, and conversely theories of the Self, abound in the production of knowledge (Anidjar 2003, xii–xxv). Such theories are what make various explanatory models possible, and both these theories and models subsequently lead to how "facts" are generated, processed, and understood. The various historical contexts in which knowledge is created reveal specific social, political, and economic factors, all of which contribute, not just coincidentally, to the emergence and subsequent acceptance of how the world works (Lockman 2004a, 3). As such, the structures – rhetorical, ideological, ontological – that make the academic study of Islam possible is my primary concern in what follows.

In Chapter 1, I attempt to begin at the beginning, with the discipline's formation in Weimar Germany. In particular I focus on two works, one composed at this time and the other much later in America, written at different moments in the genesis of the academic study of Islam, but that I contend get to heart of the current impasse. Using Abraham Geiger's *Was hat Mohammed aus dem Judenthume aufgenommen?* ("What Did Muhammad Take from Judaism?") as a metonym for the earliest German (-Jewish) scholarship devoted to Islam, I attempt to show how this scholarship was certainly not disinterested, but often part of a larger program to underscore the liberal spirit of Judaism as reflected in post-Hegelian categories. I immediately juxtapose this work with Said's highly ideological *Orientalism*, a study that still pretty much functions as one of the main works of both "theory and method" and historiography in the discipline. As interesting as his literary argument may be, historically it is highly contentious. Concerned primarily with the history of the writing about the Orient in Britain and France, he circumscribes and subsequently ignores Orientalism in Germany, such as that produced by Geiger.

Here it is important to remember that the modern discipline of "Islamic studies" began in the nineteenth-century German academy, and that it developed a critical methodological apparatus that, thanks to Said's critique, has largely fallen out of favor. As a Palestinian and as the main spokesperson for Palestinian independence in the West, Said, for whatever reason or reasons, all but wrote the Jewish contribution out of the main narrative of Islamic studies. This chapter will try to write this contribution back in, with an eye to posing and answering the question: Does this reintroduction make any difference to the discipline of Islamic studies today? In many ways this tension is emblematic of a confessional, apologetic approach to Islamic data on the one hand, and more social-scientific methods on the other. This tension, I suggest, is currently crippling the discipline.

In Chapter 2, I refocus on the formation and development of interdisciplinary Middle Eastern studies programs that occurred in the aftermath of the Second World War. My interest here is twofold. First, to show the various financial and institutional agencies that are responsible for putting funding in place to make disciplinary or interdisciplinary fields possible. Too often such issues are overlooked and we operate as though we actually encounter data as part and parcel of the natural order of things. Secondly, I am interested in the various techniques associated with socio-nationalist identity construction, in both contemporary and historical documents, in order to show how disciplinary identities also jostle among themselves to bring data into existence.

It is within such interdisciplinary programs that experts in Islam began to differentiate themselves from their colleagues. Whereas many who inhabited Middle Eastern studies programs were interested in disciplines traditionally associated with social sciences (e.g., politics, economics), scholars of "Islamic religion" defined themselves by their ability to understand (*Verstehen*) something that they amorphously referred to as "Islamic mentalities." This moment in the discipline's formation led to the gravitation of scholars of Islam, *qua* religion, into departments of religious studies in the 1970s and 1980s, a time in which the latter was privileging essences, interiority, and the irreducible nature of religious phenomena. The relationship between Islamic studies and religious studies, however, is not necessarily a productive one. Framed initially as a series of questions: Why are experts in Islam so indifferent to issues of theory and method in the academic study of religion? Does the study of philology somehow preclude or at least create such indifference? Has the desire to escape from the charge of Orientalism led to the perhaps unintended consequence of identifying too closely with the object of study? All of these questions, in turn, will lead to the major one that will occupy me in subsequent chapters: Have the politics of personal identity and the ideology of American foreign policy led to the fragmentation of Islamic studies within the academic study of religion?

Chapter 3 follows the thread picked up in the previous chapter, and investigates the multi-pronged attacks against the discovery of "universal modes" of thought that was the object of area studies programs. As the traditionally excluded began to assail the excesses of the Enlightenment project, there followed, among other things, the increased need to take refuge from these excesses in the inner experiences, often amorphously associated with faith claims, of those studied. In this chapter, I focus on three individuals – Wilfred Cantwell Smith, Marshal G. S. Hodgson, and Fazlur Rahman – who I argue were most responsible for orientating the study of Islam towards the academic study of religion. These three scholars saw faith and experience as irreducible factors internal to individuals, and argued that such internal phenomena somehow led to the creation of various *external* cultural and social manifestations. This argument still pretty much guides the main trajectories of the discipline.

Chapter 4 provides an attempt to redirect the conversation so that it is less interested in Muslim "experience" or "experiences" and more interested in questions of rhetorical and social formations. The data that I examine in this chapter consists of various introductory textbooks used in teaching a course often generically called "Introduction to Islam." Such courses often do nothing more than describe what Muslims do (e.g., "Muslims pray five times a day, and these five prayers are called…") or at least think they do. What are the assumptions of such courses? What discourse or discourses in religion do they adopt or play into? And, most importantly, what might a course on Islam – informed by those who work on the critical discourse in religion – look like?

Chapter 5 examines the impact of 9/11 on the academic study of Islam. What happens when the scholar of medieval Islam suddenly becomes the focus of media attention? More often than not, unfortunately, she or he usually ends up speaking using essentialisms ("Islam does not condone…") or other generic and often meaningless slogans. As data, I am interested in numerous books produced by either professional Islamicists (e.g., Seyyed Hossein Nasr, John Esposito), those pretending to be (e.g., Karen Armstrong), or those who are highly critical of what they perceive to be certain fundamental and categorical failures of the discipline (e.g., Martin Kramer).

Finally, in the conclusion to this study, I move from deconstruction to construction, and argue that because of factors such as the current political situation in the US, and the lengthy history of philological skills as the prerequisite for admission into the field, there has been a real resistance on the part of Islamicists to engage in interdisciplinary conversations with other disciplines. I contend here that scholars of Islam must reach out to other disciplines, programs, area studies – to religious studies, to cultural studies, to diaspora studies, to sociology, to history, to anthropology, to political science, etc. – in order to examine Islamic cultures in as wide a web as possible.

Let me conclude this introduction on a somewhat optimistic note. We have to remember that the academic study of Islam within departments of religious studies is probably no more that twenty-five or thirty years old. Because of this there is much room for intellectual growth, migration into new areas, and florescences *that could be* brought about by conversations with other departments or disciplinary programs. My only concern is that these avenues may not be explored given the extremely political and highly charged ideological nature of the current global moment. Islamic studies must, in short, resist the temptation, as so many have done in the past, to move towards interiority at the expense of socio-cultural formations, of understanding at the expense of explanation. What follows, then, attempts to chart a course, admittedly only one of many possible courses, for a future that is aware of its past, and a past that only makes sense through the contingencies of the present and the future.

1 Loss of Memory, Loss of Focus: Geiger, Said, and the Search for Missing Origins

> What then is truth? A mobile army of metaphors, metonyms, and anthropomorphisms – in short, a sum of human relations, which have been enhanced, transposed, and embellished poetically and rhetorically, and which after long use seem firm, canonical, and obligatory to a people: truths are illusions about which one has forgotten that is what they are; metaphors which are worn out and without sensuous power; coins which have lost their pictures and now matter only as metal, no longer as coins (Nietzsche 1954 [1873], 46–47).

In a series of acrimonious exchanges occurring in a number of venues in the 1980s, including *The New York Review of Books*, Edward Said and Bernard Lewis debated the merits of the scholarly enterprise of Islamic studies. Lewis charged that Said's thesis in *Orientalism* was "tendentious," "arbitrary," "reckless," and "not merely false but absurd" (1982a, 51–52). Even "the one Arabic phrase which he quotes," argues Lewis, "is misspelled and mistranslated" (1982a, 53). To these charges, Said responds that Lewis's attacks are "superficial," based on his own "insecurity," and that while his Arabic may be okay, Lewis possesses "carelessness in reading English" (1982, 44–45). Said subsequently equates Lewis with anti-Arab radicals such as Meir Kahane, the Israeli political party Gush Emunim, and accuses Lewis of reproducing "the Zionist vision of the world divided into racial and ethnic ghettos" (1982, 46). Not to be outdone, Lewis subsequently responds that the tragedy of *Orientalism* is "that it takes a general problem, and reduces it to the level of political polemic and personal abuse" (1982b, 48).

Welcome to the field of Islamic studies.

Taking this anecdote as my point of departure, this chapter examines, briefly yet critically, a key moment in the formation of Islamic studies: The 1835 publication of Abraham Geiger's *Was hat Mohammed aus dem Judenthume aufgenommen?* Despite its unfortunate title, translated literally into English as "What did Muhammad take from Judaism?" this work is nonetheless a milestone, providing one of the earliest positive treatments of Muhammad in a European vernacular, and establishing an important methodological framework for contextualizing early Islam. My interest here is not so much to debate the merits of the work, the truth or accuracy of its claims, but to contextualize it within specific and contemporaneous religious, intellectual, and ideological trajectories. Such an exercise should provide an interesting segue into a particular scholarly discourse devoted to situating Islam. By articulating a sustained discussion of Geiger's treatise, this chapter seeks to lay bare some of the extra-scholarly issues that went into the creation, discovery, and taxonomy of "Islamic data" in the earliest years of the discipline's formation.

Only by understanding the genealogy of the metaphors, tropes, vocabularies, and categories of one's discipline can one understand how it manufactures knowledge, thereby determining what will be found to be of significance or not. Such a genealogical acknowledgement, however, need not imply tacit endorsement of its first principles. In this regard, and as the passage from Nietzsche that opens this chapter implies, all discourses are ultimately constructed with political claims and ideological implications often disguised as theoretical innovations, with assumptions of knowledge and wills to power masquerading as metaphysical truths. By ferreting out such assumptions and implications we can confront and subsequently dismantle both the intellectual and extra-intellectual baggage bequeathed to us by our predecessors. This necessarily gives rise to an important set of questions: What should remain in the new discipline of Islamic studies? Who decides what is outmoded or not? The answers to such questions are themselves highly contentious and cannot, nor will not, be free from further ideological considerations.

As we shall see in this chapter, it is often all too easy to accuse those with whom one disagrees as having an agenda, all the while ignoring one's own, or at the very least those that are implicit in the disciplinary jargon inherited from others. It is these agendas and counter-agendas, as I argued in the introductory chapter, that have the potential to buckle in on one another, sounding the death-knell of the discipline. Rather than contend that one group's theory is correct and another's flawed, it becomes necessary to question the entire set of assumptions bequeathed to us, and upon which the foundations of a set of critical discourses known as Islamic studies rest. There are problems that attend every discourse; yet, unless we become aware of these problems, we will not only mimic the same arguments, but continue to make the same categorical mistakes. Moreover, as I have argued in another context, there are many positive reasons for engaging in such disciplinary soul-searching:

> Any attempt to take stock of our discipline, no matter how incomplete or problematic, tells us something about the fate of our field, the sociology of our knowledge, and, perhaps more disconcertingly, our collective fate as practitioners of a critical discourse. Because this critical discourse neither fell from heaven nor appeared *ex nihilo*, the interrogation of its prime matter, the very stuff of its constitutive parts, is not only required, but necessary for the well-

being and continued viability of what we do or of what we imagine it is that we do (Hughes 2006, 564).

Rather than remain solely in the nineteenth century, the period of formation, this chapter refracts one particular genealogical discussion through the prism of Said's well-known critique of Orientalism. This refraction allows me to move the discussion from simple historical interest to a broader analysis that illuminates several of the major issues at stake in the current application of Islamic studies. This approach involves negotiating several disciplinary and ideological minefields. In the post-9/11 world, various antagonistic constituencies – from political neo-conservatives to Islamic essentialists – invoke the thought of Said, whether to show how it is sympathetic to Islamic terror (e.g., Kramer 2001) or a panacea to understanding the ills of colonialism and its intellectual baggage (e.g., Lockman 2004a). These radically different readings are ultimately irreconcilable, and my goal here is certainly not to take sides by either writing Said's hagiography or obituary. My aim, on one level much simpler, is to argue that Said's account is as fraught with political and ideological assumptions and consequences as that of the Orientalism that he sought to demolish. Unless we face up to this legacy, realizing that *Orientalism* is decidedly *not* a work of historiography, it becomes very difficult to move forward. A disciplinary edifice constructed solely on a Saidian foundation, in other words, produces as fragile a structure as that designed and constructed by Orientalism. The thread that begins here will be picked up more fully in Chapter 5, where I will show that the current debates of neo-cons and Islamic apologists simply, unabashedly, and often uninterestingly replay the Said–Lewis debates mentioned at the beginning of this chapter.

The argument that I trust will slowly emerge in the present chapter is that Islam emerged at a particular moment in the nineteenth-century Germany Academy through a critical discourse known as Oriental studies. This, of course, is not tantamount to saying that Islam is a figment of our collective imagination, only that we have all too easily created a rubric into which we often lazily ascribe a perceived stable and essential phenomenon to which we assign any number of properties that can neatly coincide with or become antagonistic towards an equally reified "us" or "self." In the modern period, this Islam is often neatly packaged as a threat to our collective identity (see the discussion in McCutcheon 2005, 47–52). In many ways, this is not significantly different from the earliest scholarly discourses devoted to Islam, which although equally essentialist, tended to be more concerned with constructing a Semitic group (the defining feature of which was Judaism) that could be neatly reified and subsequently removed from an equally problematic Aryan one (Conrad 1999, 138–42).

Islam thus often became undifferentiated from, and in many ways an extension of, a Semitic Judaism. This conflation of Judaism and Islam, as opposed to their juxtaposition today, produced interesting results as many of the earliest scholars of Islam, themselves Jews, argued for a positive treatment of Islam. Yet, although Islam was ultimately perceived to be little more than a corrupted form of Judaism, it was nonetheless understood historically as a religious tradition that had allowed Jews to thrive. Since Jews, in early and middle nineteenth-century Germany, were prohibited from teaching at German universities and holding similar jobs in the civil service, this Islam became a positively constructed prism with which to filter virtues such as tolerance, inclusion, and the appreciation of difference.

In order to highlight the Jewish angle on the formation of the critical discourse of Islamic studies, I have chosen to focus, as mentioned earlier, on Abraham Geiger. My goal in doing this is not solely for historical accuracy nor to re-include a discourse that I feel has been unduly erased in works that claim to be genealogical. Although these two features are certainly important to me, I also engage in this enterprise in order to illumine, using a different light, a contemporary debate. Islamic studies at the beginning of the twenty-first century, like its cognate disciplines Middle Eastern studies or Near Eastern studies, is currently wracked by the conflicts in the Middle East. This political crisis, as will become clearer in subsequent chapters, is omnipresent, regardless of whether one's area of specialty is contemporary politics or medieval law. Because of features such as the Islamophobic atmosphere on college campuses or the desire to speak to the media, the specialist on Islam often is more than just a scholar, but a mouthpiece for a particular religion (regardless of whether he or she is actually a Muslim).

My goal, in returning to the nineteenth century, is not only wistful, to show that things could have been otherwise, but also critical. That is, because of the current conflicts in the Middle East, the reified contemporary construction between Jew and Arab (Anidjar 2003, xxii–xxv), it has become all too easy and comfortable to write off the Jewish contribution to Islamic studies. Given the role of the Middle East in shaping the current discourse of Islamic studies, I hope to show how contemporary political concerns often masquerade themselves as critical scholarship done under the guise of objectivity. Shorn of such guises, however, what remains, as the passage from Nietzsche so powerfully demonstrates, is ideology.

In what follows I proceed by looking at two different constructions, both of which briefly emerge in the fault lines of the debate between Said and Lewis, but which may be quickly overshadowed by the heated nature of the polemics involved therein. I begin with an examination of

1 Loss of Memory, Loss of Focus

one of the earliest scholarly European works *to take seriously* Islam, and its prophet, Muhammad. Although from the perspective of the twenty-first century it might seem misguided or hopelessly outdated, it was a work that proved instrumental in establishing the field of Islamic studies. This work, *Was hat Mohammed aus dem Judenthume aufgenommen?*, subsequently translated into English with the innocuous title *Judaism and Islam*,[1] proved to be the only work that its author Abraham Geiger (1810–1874) would compose on the topic of Islam before turning his attention to the reform and liberalization of Judaism in Germany. Even though he spent his life as a rabbi and not an academic (Jews were forbidden from holding academic positions in German universities), the method that inspired this work was not significantly different from that which guided his understanding of Judaism and its role in the modern nation state.

Despite the provocative nature of Geiger's title, one searches in vain to find even a passing reference to it in Said's *Orientalism*, his stinging indictment of the field. One would think that such a well-known work of European Orientalism, especially one with such a suggestive title, would be perfect fodder for Said's thesis that Orientalists sought to discredit Islam by showing that it was, *inter alia*, the sum of its redactional sources. Yet Said, a Palestinian Christian whose family was displaced from Jerusalem in 1948,[2] chose to overlook the contributions of German Orientalism, much of it produced by Jews, in favor of the often far more idiosyncratic tradition of French and British Orientalism. Writing just after the Yom Kippur War (1973) and the oil embargo of the mid 1970s, Said was extremely critical of the negative portrayal of "the Arab" and "the Muslim" in American popular culture. Although I doubt that Said was anti-Semitic, he was certainly highly critical of the state of Israel.

Geiger's construction of Islam was certainly not innocent, but was embedded in the cultural context of Jews trying to gain recognition and entry into a German society that was largely impervious to such attempts. Only by contextualizing Geiger's work does it become possible to articulate some of the many voices contained within the disciplinary formation of Islamic studies. Yet, this articulation risks erasure if we mistake, as too many do, Said's literary work for one of historiography. Although Said contends that he was not interested in German Orientalism owing to its dearth of colonial holdings (e.g., 1978, 19), the fact remains that such a decision caused him to overlook the most serious and engaged nineteenth-century scholarship devoted to Islam. This decision, I contend, was not innocuous, but itself grounded in identity politics of the 1970s, the focus of Chapter 3.

My aim in what follows is genealogical, not constructive. For example, in hindsight it may seem easy to dismiss a work published by a Jew and entitled "What did Muhammad Take from Judaism?" or alternatively to use such a title to show how Orientalist nineteenth-century scholarship on Islam was. Yet, the reality is much more complex, and it is precisely this complexity that the present chapter seeks to open up for further scrutiny. Works such as Geiger's, when understood contextually and not simply polemically, were revolutionary because they took Islam seriously and thought that the Qur'ān – like Homer, Plato, the Hebrew Bible, the New Testament, the Vedas – should be studied using the various tools that nineteenth-century source criticism provided. The goal was not to make Islam other, but to study it in the same way as Western works and religions were being studied. Despite modern objections to the contrary, works such as Geiger's played a key role in how scholars thought about early Islam and its various contexts.

The Jewish "Discovery" of Islam[3]

The production of history is never disinterested (classic studies remain White 1978; Novick 1988). Under the guise of *Wissenschaft*, German scholars created a paradigm of the humanities (*Geisteswissenschaften*) grounded in the myth of "facts" and their objective description. This new "science" (*Wissenschaft*) of history, based as it was on the "rigorous, technical and specialized" accumulation of data (Novick 1988, 24), however, does not correspond exactly to modern notions of history. The data collected were not simply to be described and analyzed, but were often understood as the unfolding of God's plan *qua* World Spirit (*Geist*) (Hegel 1953 [1837]; von Ranke 1973 [1824–1880]). As such, the study of history was not utilitarian but intimately caught up in the attempt to construct seminal periods of the past often to rejuvenate a people or a "race" (*Volk*) in the modern period (e.g., Schelling 1966 [1803], 34–38). History thus became the means by which a *Volk* could articulate its own identity by knowing and grasping its essence, and subsequently differentiating it from equally essentialized others.

Intimately connected to this quest for essences was the notion of Idealism, which regarded ideas as the substance and motivator of history. Although such ideas are only visible in manifested forms, the World Spirit was perceived, not surprisingly, as unfolding most perfectly in Christianity. Subsequent attempts to depict a Christian and/or a German essence often coincided with carving out an ontological space for them in ways that were independent or untouched by other ethnic groups (especially that of the Jews) (Mack 2003, 1–16).[4] Although Jewish historians were critical of this attempt to sever Christianity from its Jewish sources, they nevertheless absorbed many of the assumptions of this discourse and used the same categories to create a Jewish history (Schorsch 1975, 2–9). This creation of a universal Jewish history to counter the claims of Christian and/or German history led many German-Jewish historians to Islam, especially those historical periods of Islam in which Jews lived and wrote.

Any historical "reconstruction" is based on an intricate system of presences and absences that, more often than not, privileges one reading at the expense of others (on this trope more generally, see Gold 2003). In their endeavor to re-create the Jewish past, many German-Jewish scholars attempted to make Judaism in their own ideological images. Given their negative treatment in Germany, such Jewish scholars turned their attention to Islamic periods in which Jews were seen to flourish (e.g., pre-Islamic Arabia, Muslim Spain). The primary feature driving such research was the belief that emancipation of the Jews was desirable both for the Jews themselves and also for the German state. In terms of contextualizing early Islam, the goal of German-Jewish scholarship was to show, for one thing, the Jewish matrix from which Islam, like Christianity before it, emerged. By doing this, such scholars tried to demonstrate that the essence, in the Hegelian sense, of Judaism was monotheism and that this, in turn, was responsible for the formation of other monotheistic religions.

Moreover, the positive treatment of Islam by German-Jewish scholars was meant to show that when Jews were treated well, as they were perceived to be under Islamic civilization, they were productive members of society (e.g., Schorsch 1994; Cohen 1994, ch. 1; Hughes 2005). To use the words of Martin Kramer, "a Europe respectful of Islam and Muslims was more likely to show respect for Judaism and Jews" (Kramer 1999, 3). The desire for integration of Jewish studies within German universities thus became a metaphor for general Jewish emancipation and acceptance into mainstream German society (Geiger 1836, 6).

Despite the fact that Jews were prohibited from teaching at German universities, this period ushered in a new way of thinking about Judaism as Jewish scholars engaged in a full-scale historical investigation of Jewish topics. Although they, along with their non-Jewish colleagues, claimed to be working in the objective spirit of *Wissenschaft*, their historical investigations were imbued with various ideological assumptions about the nature of history, peoplehood, and the way in which they intersected. The goal of these researches, it is important to remember, was not simply confined to the past but was intimately connected to present and future concerns (Myers 1997, 707; Mack 2003, 1–16; Mendes-Flohr 1991).

With their knowledge of Hebrew, the legal structures of rabbinic Judaism, and the perceived general florescence of Judaism under Islam, German-Jews began to play a central role in the creation and development of an idiosyncratic though generally positive study of Islam (more generally, see the comments in Lewis 1993, 142–44). Jewish scholars from diverse backgrounds – among them Geiger, Gustav Weil (1808–1889), Ignaz Goldziher (1850–1921), Joseph Horovitz (1874–1931), Heinrich Speyer (1897–1935), Paul Kraus (1904–1944), Gotthold Weil (1882–1960), and Harry Austryn Wolfson (1887–1974) – played a seminal role in the emerging fields of Quranic studies, Arabic grammar, the various social and linguistic milieux in which the Qur'ān was written, and more generally, the construction of the modern fields of Islamic science and history. Although these individuals came from diverse regions, most shared a common background in having a general rabbinic upbringing, and the subsequent desire to break from this upbringing as young men. Moreover, all shared, to varying degrees, the notion that (1) Judaism played a formative role in the construction of monotheism, something that Hegel had already signaled as the defining essence of Judaism, and (2) if Europe could understand Islam's historical tolerance to the Jews, it itself might be more tolerant to Jews in the process. Some of these individuals, and it seems that this was especially the case for Geiger, were less concerned with Islam than with creating a case study of a liberal Jewish community's contribution to society when they are allowed freedom.

This is all the more interesting when put in counterpoint with scholarship on early Islam produced by non-Jews, especially those regarded as the founders of Semitic and Orientalist studies in France. Ernst Renan (1823–1892) and Antoine-Isaac Silvestre de Sacy (1758–1838), to cite but two examples, were extremely critical of Islam, Muhammad's character, and, more generally the "Semitic mind" when compared to that of the "Indo-European" (Masuzawa 2005, 174–78; Conrad 1999, 154–62). I shall have more to say about such individuals, including Said's obsession with them, below.

Abraham Geiger: The Quest for the Jewish Substrate of Islamic Origins

Since I here use Geiger as a metonym for a particular way of situating Islam in the earliest decades of the formative period of Islamic studies, it becomes necessary to contextualize him, as an individual, against more specific historical, intellectual, and sociological forces. Abraham Geiger

1 Loss of Memory, Loss of Focus

was born into a religiously observant Jewish family – both his father and a brother were rabbis in the traditional mold[5] – in Frankfurt am Main in 1810. He was enrolled in the local *heder* ("religious school") as opposed to the secular gymnasium to which young Jews were sent for preparation to enter university studies. By all accounts he was a child prodigy who could, by the age of three, read the Bible in Hebrew, and subsequently the Mishnah by the age of four and the Gemara by six (Lassner 1999, 104; requisite biographies may be found in L. Geiger 1910; Wiener 1981; Heschel 1998, 23–49; Koltun-Fromm 2006, 1–11). Although his family was afraid that a secular education might corrupt the young Abraham, it was only a matter of time before he became interested in the secular studies associated with university education.

Despite his family's protestations, in 1829 the young Geiger enrolled at the University of Heidelberg (although he later transferred to Bonn). Like many young Jews who attended German universities, Geiger enrolled in oriental languages and general philosophy. His knowledge of Hebrew and Aramaic led him to the study of classical philology and cultural history. Most importantly for his subsequent intellectual development, however, Geiger became acquainted with other young Jews inspired by the tenets and teaching of the Enlightenment, many of whom would play a leading role in the then emerging *Wissenschaft des Judentums*, or the non-religious and social-scientific study of Judaism and the Jewish people (e.g., Myers 1995, 1997; Schorsch 1975).

Geiger quickly came to the attention of non-Jewish thinkers when as a doctoral student now at the University of Marburg, he submitted an essay in a competition sponsored by the faculty of philosophy at the University of Bonn. The competition was devoted to the subject: *Inquiratur in fontes Alcorani seu legis Mohammedicae eas qui ex Judaismo derivandi sunt* ("An enquiry into the sources of the Qur'ān derived from Judaism"). The young Geiger won the prize and his essay subsequently secured for him a doctorate from the University of Marburg in June of 1834 under the directorship of Georg Wilhelm Freytag (1788–1861), himself a disciple of the aforementioned de Sacy. In the following year Geiger enlarged and translated his dissertation from Latin into German, and published it "at the expense of the author" with the title *Was hat Mohammed aus dem Judenthume aufgenommen?*

Despite the fact that Geiger was poised to become a leading figure in the then developing field of Quranic and Islamic studies, as a Jew he was forbidden by the state authorities from taking up a teaching position at a German university unless he first converted to Christianity. This was not an option for the young Geiger, and in 1833 he was ordained as a Rabbi whereupon he served various congregations in Wiesbaden, Breslau, Frankfurt, and Berlin. In this capacity, he became one of the leading figures in the development and establishment of the emerging Reform movement in Judaism. Despite his rabbinic duties, Geiger remained active, publishing scholarly articles and monographs not on Islam but on Judaism and its perceived ability to adapt and readjust its essence in history. This latter topic was intimately connected to the liberal Jewish Reform movement: If one could show that rabbinism was not part of Judaism's essence, one could quite easily move beyond the yoke of Jewish law (*halakhah*). He published a scholarly journal, *Wissenschaftliche Zeitschrift für jüdische Theologie*, and in 1874 received a teaching position in Berlin at the newly created Hochshule für die Wissenschaft des Judentums.

Since *Was hat Mohammed aus dem Judenthume aufgenommen?* was published so early in the development of the discipline of Islamic studies, it is important to be aware of what the work does and does not, claims and cannot. It was, most importantly, a work interested in using language as a way to understand religious worldviews. Here it is important to understand that Geiger's work and assumptions were intimately connected to a larger discourse contending that language played a formative role in establishing and defining the concept of Volkishness (Lincoln 1999, 47, 54–61). In this regard, nineteenth-century theories of language were intimately connected to the essence of a people: Language was perceived to define how a group (*Volk*) engaged the world and imagined reality and its alternatives. If the scholar could understand the origins of a language, or at least its defining characteristics, he could gain real insight into the mentality of the people who spoke it.

It thus becomes necessary to connect Geiger's work to the then-emerging interest in languages, especially their ontological and epistemological properties. According to Kippenberg, this interest witnessed a turn

> away from the assumption of a rational theory of language, toward the comparison of languages in order to discover its educational potential. Nothing was left of the old concept of a proto language except a common human competence to form a picture of the world independent of all external constraints (2002, 39).

The comparative analysis of language was just beginning to function as a model for the emerging study of religion. Prior to Max Müller's famous pronouncement in 1870 linking language, myth and race, German scholars such as J. G. Herder and W. von Humboldt had already theorized about the importance of language and the various ways in which humans encounter and structure reality. To quote from Kippenberg again:

> When words are communicated, they make something subjective objective and thus establish a worldview in thought. While weaving a worldview through their use of language, men weave themselves into a web at the same time. This view

continued to exercise an effect in nineteenth-century Germany for some time (2002, 40).

For Geiger, language was instrumental in ascertaining genetic affinities between religions in close geographical proximity. On the level of ideology, as a new religion is created and subsequently develops it is forced to tap into earlier truth claims, themselves expressed through pre-established lexemes deployed in surrounding religious contexts. This adoption and adaptation of technical lexemes subsequently provides the adherents of the new religion with a familiar message. Geiger further argued that such "borrowing" would be desirable when the new religion sought to proselytize or make inroads among older religions. In the case of Islam and Judaism:

> [Muhammad] hoped to strengthen the opinion that he was taught by direct revelation from God; he had also a strong wish to win over the Jews to his kingdom of faithful upon earth, and then, too, the legends and fanciful sayings of the Jews harmonized with his poetic nature (Geiger 1970 [1835], 21).

What might most surprise the modern reader of Geiger is his unwillingness to accept the Muslim view that God is the author of the Qur'ān. We have grown accustomed at the present moment of the discipline's development to use the phrase "the Qur'ān says" and not "Muhammad says" or "Muhammad, in the Qur'ān, says." Geiger, a Jewish Reformer who would have been critical of the traditional concept of *Torah min-Sinai* ("Torah from Sinai") in his own tradition, was not about to make an exception for the revelatory moment in Islam. As such, he assumes, as was customary in nineteenth-century Orientalism, that Muhammad was the author of the Qur'ān (e.g., 1970 [1835], 22–25).

In particular, Geiger argues that Muhammad used certain biblical lexemes and mythemes in order to authenticate his own message in such a manner that would also differentiate this message from earlier sources (e.g., Geiger 1835, 21–25). He argues that one of the main ways that the message of Islam caught on was not because of the genius of Muhammad, but because the populace of seventh-century Arabia was familiar with a number of monotheistic terms that Muhammad had recast from Jewish sources. Although, on one level, this argument might strike us as patronizing, historically it is probably not that far from the truth: The Quranic message, after all, does not claim to be original, but simply the recasting of an Ur-message in Arabic.

Geiger's methodology, as was fairly customary in German scholarship of the period, revolved around language, especially its ability to vector ideological and emotive sentiment. For him, the key to contextualizing Islam, as indeed it would later be for his understanding Judaism, was based on the necessity of understanding religious texts within their immediate historical, intellectual, and social milieux. In his work on the Qur'ān, he took what he thought were Arabic technical terms – e.g., *tābūt* ("ark"), *tawrāt* ("torah"), *jannah* ("garden"), and *sakīnah* ("divine presence") – and tried to show how they were derived from Hebrew and Aramaic words. His operating assumption was that:

> as the ushering in of hitherto unknown religious conceptions is always marked by the introduction of new words for their expression, and as the Jews in Arabia, even when able to speak Arabic, kept to the Rabbinical Hebrew names for their religious conceptions; so words which from their derivation are shown to be not Arabic but Hebrew, or better still Rabbinic, must be held to prove the Jewish origin of the conceptions expressed (1970 [1835], 30–31).

There are a number of problems with this thesis. For one thing, despite the fact that there exist many similarities between Arabic and Hebrew, Geiger in retrospect was unable to demonstrate that this was tantamount to a conscious "borrowing" on the part of Muhammad. Moreover, similarities between the two languages might well be due to common Semitic roots as opposed to one religio-political-ethnic group consciously taking words and/or concepts from another. Yet, despite such problems, Geiger's thesis does not automatically break down. The historical record, not to mention the Qur'ān itself, documents that a large number of Jews lived in the Arabian peninsula, that they would have interacted with the nascent Muslim polity including Muhammad, and that the universal categories of monotheism would have played a large role in early Islamic speculation about God, covenant, humans, and so on.

In order to see just what is new here, it is worthwhile to show just how markedly different Geiger's thesis was when compared to contemporaneous non-Jewish accounts of Islamic origins. Such accounts produced scholarship on Islam that was highly, perhaps one could argue obsessively, subjective (e.g., Daniel 1997; Hentsch 1992). Juxtaposed against this, the methodological apparatus developed by the likes of Geiger was influenced by the emerging *Wissenschaft des Judentums* ("Science of Judaism"), and was formulated neither to undermine Islam nor to show that it was simply the sum of its sources. The aim of this new paradigm, on the contrary, was to understand the creation and development of the early Islamic polity, especially the Qur'ān, in its various historical, linguistic, social, and religious contexts. Although Geiger and others did not necessarily phrase it in such a manner, they nonetheless worked on the assumption that if they could show the genius of Islam they could reveal the beauty of Judaism behind it.

1 Loss of Memory, Loss of Focus

Despite the politically incorrect title of Geiger's work, it was – viewed from the moment of its publication – revolutionary. It provided a vocabulary and a set of categories both to understand the Qur'ān in context, and to speak about Muhammad in ways that were hitherto unheard of in Orientalist scholarship. Whereas the latter tradition had always tended to regard Muhammad as a self-serving, power-hungry, and over-sexed individual, Geiger portrays him as a religious "enthusiast" (*Schwärmer*) with noble ends:

> It is by no means to be imagined that we regard [Muhammad] as a deceiver who deceived intentionally, and with a well-weighed consideration of each step as to whether or not it would help him toward his aim of deluding others. Wahl regards him in this light. On the contrary, *we must guard ourselves carefully against such an opinion, and look upon it as a sign of persistent prejudice and total misunderstanding of the human heart. Muhammad seems rather to have been a genuine enthusiast (Schwärmer) who was himself convinced of his divine mission, and to whom the union of all religions appeared necessary to the welfare of mankind* (1970 [1835], 24–25; my italics).

Geiger argues that Muhammad consciously looked to the Jews when he established his own religion (Pearlman 1970, vii–xxiv; Lassner 1999, 106–18). Since Muhammad would not have had direct access to Jewish texts, the subsequent message of the Qur'ān in particular, and Islam in general, is, according to his reading, ultimately a distortion of Jewish themes that nevertheless enabled Muhammad to authenticate his message (1970 [1835], 17–21). This is certainly not to say that Geiger was convinced of either the veracity or truthfulness of Muhammad's message, only the intensity of his belief:

> Of course, even in the most fanatical minds there are occasional lucid intervals, and during these Muhammad certainly deceived himself and others; it is also undeniable that at times ambition and love of power were the incentives to his actions, *but even so the harsh judgment generally passed upon him is unjustifiable* (1970 [1835], 25; my italics).

The work was reviewed favorably by Silvestre de Sacy, the teacher of Geiger's own *Doktorvater*, who wrote of the work that it "renders almost superfluous all the preceding discussion which I would call prejudicial" (quoted in Lassner 1999, 106). Yet, he is also quick to criticize Geiger for his overgenerous praise of Muhammad, and instead preferred to refer to the prophet of Islam as a "skilled imposter, premeditated in all his actions and cold-bloodedly evaluating all that which favored and assured the success of his ambitious projects" (quoted in Lassner 1999, 107). In the place of such constructions, Geiger claimed that Muhammad had been treated too harshly by European scholarship, something that the sources themselves cannot and do not support (Geiger 1835, 25). J. L. Fleischer (1801–1888), the leading German Arabist of the second half of the nineteenth century, wrote positively: "I give my sincerest thanks to Dr. Geiger for the wealth of new and valuable data gleaned from his book" (Fleischer 1841, 107). One of the greatest Semitists and Arabists of the early twentieth century, Theodor Nöldeke (1836–1930), called Geiger's revised dissertation "an epoch-making work whose findings rapidly became the common stock of scholarship" (Nöldeke 1938, 208–10, quoted in Pearlmann 1970, xi). Moreover, he argued that an up-to-date revision of the work in addition to fresh work on the subject was an urgent desideratum within the field of Islamic studies.

It is also important to note that Geiger, as can be witnessed in the last block quote cited above, could be very disparaging of Muhammad and Islam (e.g., 1835, 3–6). Yet, even his critical statements must be put in counterpoint with those made by the likes of Renan and other Orientalists; secondly, as I have tried to argue all along, more was going on in Geiger's work than just disinterested scholarship on Islam, Muhammad, and the Qur'ān. At stake for Geiger was Judaism's role in the origins and subsequent development of monotheisms, and how Judaism played a formative role in the rise of Islam and, going even further back, Christianity.

In terms of Quranic scholarship, Geiger's approach was equally new. Unwilling to regard Islam's sacred scripture as a morass of hastily incomprehensible sayings and phrases, Geiger tried to uncover the way in which terms, and the religious connotations that they vectored, became embedded in Islam's sacred scripture. How does the Qur'ān employ such terms? How does it change them? Why might it change them? These questions, in many ways, are still very modern, and ones that need to be asked in order to establish and understand the contexts of earliest Islamic cultures.

Islam and Contemporary Jewish Concerns

We get an even better sense of what Geiger was up to when we put the aforementioned work in counterpoint with some of his later writings. Although he would always remain interested in the Jewish-Arabic historical relationship, he never again published anything solely devoted to Islam or the Qur'ān; instead, he focused his attention primarily on Judaism, including a two-volume work entitled in English translation *Judaism and Its History*. For Geiger, the formation of Islam in seventh-century

1 Loss of Memory, Loss of Focus

Arabia provides a window onto a barely perceptible feature of Jewish history:

> [Muhammad] received those truths [of monotheism]; he was not their creator, he simply took them over out of Judaism. The rise of Islam reveals to us a fragment of Jewish history which would have remained entirely hidden for us, without it (Geiger 1985 [1865], 254).

Just as Judaism provided the matrix out of which Christianity emerged, it also functions as the "wet nurse" of Islam's arrival:

> Thus Judaism, if not the mother of Islam as it is of Christianity, is yet its nurse that nourished it with her best forces, yet its teacher that fitted out the pupil and raised him. Did the fosterchild treat his nurse with kinder feeling than the daughter showed to her mother? In the beginning it had that appearance... The treasures of knowledge are again raised and are turned to good account for Moslems as well as for those living among them... Thus Islam requites, even if not with friendly, kind feeling, but yet by the new energy which it pours forth, to Judaism what it has borrowed, and partly amends the wrong done to it (1985 [1865], 258–59).

Here Geiger is particularly interested in the relative freedom that Islam showed to the Jews, especially when compared to medieval Christendom. As I have argued elsewhere (2005, 59–62), he was particularly interested in Muslim Spain:

> Islam rendered great service to Judaism by leaving to it room; it did not go in advance of it in everything and could not offer everything to it, but it gave it room for the development of its powers. And thus we look back upon that illustrious time as a brilliant period of Judaism (Geiger 1985 [1865], 352).

Implicit here of course is not only a criticism of medieval Christianity, but, more pointedly, a criticism of the German authorities of his own day. If Jews are not persecuted and are given room to develop, they will become productive members of society, producing individuals with the magnitude of Maimonides or ibn Gabirol (Hughes 2005, 51–52).

The scholarship that German-Jewish scholars of early Islam bequeathed to us, despite some of its obvious lacunae and limitations, is not simply a historical relic. Rather, the methodological assumptions developed by scholars such as Geiger created a number of features that are now regarded as commonplace, e.g., that we should take Muhammad seriously, that Islam is a real religion. Moreover, they also provided a critical vocabulary with which to analyze the Qur'ān. For example, what words, categories, and motifs does the Qur'ān recycle from earlier scriptures? Does it employ them in the same manner? If not, how does it potentially subvert that which came before in order to authenticate its new message? In this regard, scholars like Geiger who tried to show the Qur'ān's dependence on biblical and rabbinic sources made the important discovery that words are not innocent, but that ideas often ride on the backs of such terms. Certainly there is much in the work of Geiger that is wrong, outdated, and, from today's perspective, based on faulty premises. Yet, some of the questions that he asked and the modes of analysis that he employed remain important to our understanding of Islamic origins.

The Orientalist Critique

Although the role of identity politics in the shaping of the modern discourse on Islamic studies will be the subject of several of the following chapters, it becomes necessary to examine the critique that Orientalism, beginning in the 1970s, has leveled against the so-called philological-textual tradition of the discipline that we witness in works like those produced by Geiger. An unfortunate byproduct of this critique is that it has become all too easy to write off critical scholarship on Islamic origins or the Qur'ān as Orientalist, thus tainting such scholarship as somehow invested if not in physical empire maintenance then at least in the academic imperialism over others. This, of course, is certainly not to imply that important work on Islamic origins is not still carried out, only that for the most part it tends to be done in Europe and Israel (an important exception is Rippin, e.g., 2001b), and rarely if ever in religious studies (an important exception is Berg 2000, 2003).

Even before the publication of Edward Said's highly influential *Orientalism* (1978), there had already emerged a growing dissatisfaction and subsequent critique of the field (e.g., Owen 1973; Asad 1973; Laroui 1976). Yet despite such early indictments, by far the strongest charge emerged from the pen of Said. Basing himself on the theoretical foundations laid out by Michel Foucault that knowledge of "x" was tantamount to power over "x," Said, probably owing to the fact that he was a literary theorist and neither a philologist not Orientalist by training, was able to reach out to scholars in a wide array of disciplines, in addition to a number of constituencies outside of the Academy.

Said defines Orientalism in the following manner:

> Orientalism is a style of thought based upon an ontological and epistemological distinction made between "the Orient" and (most of the time) "the Occident." Thus a very large mass of writers, among whom are poets, novelists, philosophers, political theorists, economists, and imperial administrators, have accepted the basic distinction between East and West as the starting point for elaborate

1 Loss of Memory, Loss of Focus

theories, epics, novels, social descriptions, and political accounts concerning the Orient, its peoples, customs, "mind," destiny, and so on (1978, 2–3).

The study of the Orient in general and Islam in particular, then, was not simply about the innocent production of knowledge, but about a way of thinking about and ultimately constructing Self and Other. This way of thinking was, in turn, inextricably bound up in the will to power of Europe (and subsequently America and Israel) over the East and all that is Eastern. Said's main argument is that the vocabularies and the categories supplied by all late nineteenth- and early twentieth-century scholarship (in addition to literature, opera, etc.) on the Orient is inherently political, an attempt to create an inverse opposite by which the West creates an other, "the Orient," to define itself, its values and characteristics, better (e.g., Said 1978, 15–20).[6] According to this critique, knowledge of the East is tantamount to power over it, and Orientalist scholarship exists in the service of Empire to sustain Western hegemony. Said's critique proved to be so damaging that the field, in many respects, has never really recovered, evidence of which may be gleaned from the fact that virtually every single department of Oriental studies in North American universities underwent name changes during the 1980s.

The fallout, both positive and negative, from the publication of *Orientalism* has been severe. Viewed positively, Said's work is extremely suggestive in forcing us to attune ourselves to the language we use to think about and imagine other cultures. Linguistic and ontological categories are not always as innocuous as they seem, but often carry with them implicit wills to power. This has forced many, though by no means all, to become more self-reflective of the various ways we conceptualize Islam and Islamic data. Here, however, we must remember that this is not what Geiger was doing. Like Said, he sought to show the limitations and prejudices of an existing discourse. Unlike Said, though, he proposed an actual solution to attempt to move beyond the methodological impasse.

However, when viewed from another angle, the critique of Orientalism has had the unfortunate notion of curtailing certain avenues of scholarly activity. The result is that it has been all too easily to dismiss, often without even reading, the work of scholars mentioned in the previous section as inherently biased and chock full of various essentialisms. In its most simple form this can be paraphrased in the following way: Muslims sources speak of the Qur'ān as the word of God, Orientalists are interested in the Jewish and other sources of the Qur'ān; therefore Orientalists seek to construct an Islam that is contingent upon Judeo-Christian ideas. I shall return to this topic in greater detail in Chapter 5.

This ambiguity of the Saidian legacy, it seems to me, is embedded in an unfortunate oversight that resides at the heart of *Orientalism*. How much of an issue one wants to make of this oversight, however, is in turn dependent upon how much one has invested in the Saidian critique. Because Said has warned us that all academic knowledge is tainted by the political and the ideological, it is necessary to ask why he would completely ignore the German tradition of Orientalism in favor of that produced by the French and British. His rationale is that:

> I had to focus rigorously upon the British-French and later the American material because it seemed to me inescapably true not only that Britain and France were the pioneer nations in the Orient and in Oriental studies, but that these vanguard positions were held by virtue of the two greatest colonial networks in pre-twentieth-century history (1978, 17).

While certainly no other European countries had either the colonial holdings or the imperial aspirations of the British and the French, it is highly contentious that these two countries were the pioneer nations in developing Oriental and/or Islamic studies. Yet, in focusing his analysis on these two countries, Said overlooks the most serious scholarly tradition devoted to Oriental studies, a tradition that was often much more quotidian, and, as I argued in the previous section, provides the genealogy of the modern study of Islamic studies (not to mention South Asian studies, etc.). Said's rationale for leaving out this tradition of scholarship is that:

> I believe that the sheer quality, consistency, and mass of British, French, and American writing on the Orient lifts it above the doubtless crucial work done in Germany, Italy, Russia, and elsewhere. But I think it is also true that the major steps in Oriental scholarship were first taken in either Britain and France, and then elaborated upon by Germans (1978, 17–18).

Yet, if we are to take Said's claim seriously that knowledge is tantamount to power, and that no scholarship can be innocent of certain claims to ideology, what are we to make of such an omission? Why, for example, lump in the German scholarly tradition on the Orient with that of the Italians and the Russians, two traditions that are not nearly as important to the genesis of the discipline? Indeed, Said subsequently admits:

> Any work that seeks to provide an understanding of academic Orientalism and pays little attention to scholars like Steinthal, Müller, Becker, Goldziher, Brockelmann, Nöldeke – to mention only a handful – needs to be reproached, and I freely reproach myself (1978, 18).

Here Said no longer groups the Germans with the Italians, the Russians, and "others," but freely admits that any attempt to understand "*academic*" writings on the Orient must take into consideration the German tradition. So why does he ignore it? Answers could range from the innocuous, *viz.*, it didn't suit his polemical intent so he bypassed it (e.g.,

1 Loss of Memory, Loss of Focus

Rodinson 1987, 131 n. 3), to the ideological, viz., that the major players in German Orientalism were primarily Jews and that in ignoring them Said writes them out of the discipline's history (e.g., Lewis 1993; Lassner 1999).

Regardless of Said's intent, the fact remains that his critique has largely made the German tradition of Orientalism guilty by association with the French and the British. For example, Said makes Renan a metonym for the entire European Orientalist tradition. For Said, Renan refined and systematized the Orientalist discourse created by de Sacy, something that, he argues, has remained essentially static from "the late 1840s to the present in the United States" (Said 1978, 17–18). This discourse subsequently becomes the driving force of the political apparatus that seeks and achieves power over the Orient. From France, this discourse is subsequently imported to the "Austro-German school of Orientalism," and therefore all European Orientalists can, in one way or another, be genealogically traced back to Renan and Silvestre de Sacy (Said 1980, 110–11; although see the useful comments in Conrad 1999, 138–42). It is, thus, fairly transparent what Said is doing: if one can discredit Renan and de Sacy, one can dismiss the entire European and American tradition of Orientalism as biased, racist, and subjective. It is worth noting in this respect that Ignaz Goldziher, the great Hungarian-Jewish Orientalist, whose works are reprinted in English translation to this day, was extremely critical of Renan and his vision of the Orient and the quiddity of Islamic studies (Conrad 1999, 145–48).

So even though Said spends considerable time on the likes of Renan and de Sacy, he completely ignores the main figures who were ultimately responsible for defining the parameters of the modern academic study of Islam: Geiger, Weil, Horovitz, and especially Goldziher. These individuals engaged in the historical and linguistic (re)construction of early Islam, showing how Muhammad and the Qur'ān fitted into broader religious, intellectual, and philological contexts of late antique Arabia. This was an analysis that was not based on a general ahistorical methodology, but one that revolved around source criticism, comparative philology, morphology, and syntax – features that are the hallmark of a social-scientific approach to other sacred scriptures. So despite the criticism that such scholars were engaged in a process of discrediting Islam by making it other, the case was the exact opposite: these scholars engaged in a systematic attempt to not make Islam so strange, to show how it could be analyzed using the same methods employed for the Hebrew Bible, the New Testament, the Vedas, and so on.

Although the Germans had more than their fair share of wacky racial theory, and ultimately an even deadlier telos (e.g., the Shoah), it was directed primarily against an internal Other (e.g., "the Jews") and not an external Other. Yet, when it comes to the academic study of Islam, the German-speaking tradition of Orientalism produced far more important works, many of which are still in use today, than anything produced in France or Britain.

A Clash of Paradigms

While I certainly have no intention of railing against the importance offered by critics of Orientalism (the field, not the book), one unfortunate result is that the type of historical and contextual approach to the Qur'ān, especially its emphasis on possible Judaic sources, homologues or substrata, can be too easily dismissed by the charge of "Orientalism." This has created, especially in Islamic studies that radiates from North American departments of religious studies, a situation in which we witness the dismantling of a historical and critical apparatus that attempts to contextualize the Qur'ān (for exceptions, though not so much in religious studies, see Crone 1987; Crone and Cook 1977; Wansbrough 1977, 2001; one exception in religious studies is the essays in Berg 2000, 2003) and, in its place, the establishment of an amorphous, essentialist, and ahistorical methodology.[7] Attempts to examine the Qur'ān – its use of, reliance on, and difference from other writings – in various ancient Near Eastern contexts are now often regarded as a political act to undermine the Qur'ān and, by extension, Islam. The situation becomes even more convoluted since Said, a Palestinian-American, becomes highly critical of what he perceives to be a Western, and implicitly Zionist, attempt to gain political hegemony over a misrepresented Islam:

> Orientalism governs Israeli policy towards the Arabs throughout, as the recently published Koenig Report amply proves. There are good Arabs (the ones who do as they are told) and bad Arabs (who do not, and are therefore terrorists). Most of all there are all those Arabs who, once defeated, can be expected to sit obediently behind an infallibly fortified line, manned by the smallest possible number of men, on the theory that the Arabs have had to accept the myth of Israeli superiority and will never dare attack (1978, 306–307).

Here we must situate Said's comments. A Palestinian Christian from Jerusalem who, like many other Palestinian families, either left or were forced to flee (dependent upon which side one chooses to ask) when fighting broke out between Arabs and Jews in 1947, not to mention that the subsequent Six-Day War (1967) saw Jerusalem come under Israeli control. Finally, the years immediately preceding the publication of

1 Loss of Memory, Loss of Focus

Orientalism witnessed the Yom-Kippur War in 1973. It is against this backdrop of flight and displacement, Israeli and Arab aggression, war and death, that Said wrote his *magnum opus*. I certainly have no intention of engaging in cheap psychoanalysis here; indeed, when it comes to Said more than enough of this has already been done. Nor do I have any intention of reducing his complex argument to simple material causes. I do think it important, however, that Said's antagonism to Israel is undeniable and that this antagonism played a large role in shaping his argument about how Europe has manufactured "the Orient" in general, and "Arabs" and "Muslims" in particular. As a result, Said was naturally drawn to the farfetched accounts of the likes of Renan and de Sacy, but largely ignored the much more sober-minded scholarship of the likes of Goldziher or Geiger.

If this were simply an historical argument, we could state the case and move on. Yet, as I argued at the beginning of this chapter, genealogies live on even when individuals are dead and buried. The assumptions, presuppositions, and prejudices of such genealogies insinuate themselves into the mainframe and emerge at the most unlikely of places. Although the tension between these two, for lack of a better term, approaches may have come to a head in the Lewis–Said exchange with which I began this chapter, these tensions, as we shall see in Chapter 5, reverberate into the present. In many ways, the chapters that follow will revisit this "genealogical struggle," time and again. Yet, to stay with the main argument of this chapter for just a little longer, the most unfortunate by-product of the current *Kulturkampf* has been that those who employ the contextual historical and literary approach to the Qur'ān are often all too easily written off by the now pejorative term "Orientalist." Whether or not it has been intentional, I am worried that there has been a tendency to lump scholars like Geiger in with either nineteenth-century racist scholarship (like that of Renan) or with contemporary Islamophobia.

Here it might be worth introducing the comments of Joseph Horovitz, professor at the University of Frankfurt and subsequent head of the Oriental studies department at the Hebrew University in Jerusalem. Writing in 1925, roughly ninety years after the publication of Geiger's *Was hat Mohammed aus dem Judenthume aufgenommen?*, he comments:

> It is over ninety years since A. Geiger attempted to answer the question, "What did Muhammad take over from Judaism?" Since then, it is true, numerous details dealing with the subject have been supplemented, but no other comprehensive treatment of the theme was undertaken. It is self-evident that the unaltered reprint of Geiger's work cannot present us with a picture of the present-day status of research…because the methodological hypotheses on the basis of which

the work would have to be approached today have undergone decided changes (Horovitz 1925, 145).

Geiger's work, in other words, is not the final word on Islamic origins. As in any discipline, one would expect methodologies to change, develop, and be refined over a one hundred year period. Those German and German-Jewish scholars who came after Geiger saw the limitations of his method, but they did so on philological and historical grounds, not on political or ideological ones. So, modern accounts that label Geiger's method as "extreme" and "polemical" are, I would argue, inaccurate.[8] We must not lose sight of the pioneering research of Geiger, especially when put in its historical context. German-Jewish scholars writing after Geiger, such as Horovitz (1925), Speyer (1931), and others (e.g., Hirschfeld 1878; Schapiro 1907) were often critical of Geiger's work, but the point I wish to make here is that they did not see the need to desist from examining the various philological and historical contexts that vector and are vectored in the Qur'ān. Rather, as is the case with the development of any discipline, their goal was to push earlier ideas in new directions to fit the evidence as it comes to light. This approach, I contend, must continue to fuel the discipline today.

Conclusions

Although the literary-philological methodological approach to the Qur'ān would be in vogue until roughly the Second World War, it gradually fell out of favor for a variety of reasons. This is not the place to trace the various paradigm shifts in intellectual circles; however, let me briefly comment on the gradual effacement of the Jewish contribution to Quranic studies in particular and Islamic studies in general. As Jews were forced out of academic positions during the Nazi era, Jewish contributions to the arts and sciences were generally written out of Germany's dominant narrative. This may be witnessed most clearly in the historiographical survey of German Orientalism published in 1940 by Hans Heinrich Schaeder, a professor at the University of Berlin. Despite claims to objectivity, Schaeder does not mention one single German-Jewish scholar (Kramer 1999, 20–21; an important corrective, written after the war, is Fück 1955).

Said's desire to write German(-Jewish) scholarship out of the dominant narrative of Islamic studies by subsuming it under the French and British paradigms of Orientalism has created a situation in which the critical tools and analytical methodology developed by German Orientalism are often ignored or, even worse, regarded as politically suspect. This has created a

1 Loss of Memory, Loss of Focus

situation in many quarters of the North American academy where it becomes impolitic to speak of the Jewish presence and Jewish categories that went into the development of the Qur'ān. (And if one does this, one's work is immediately part of "Jewish studies," not "Islamic studies.") Fortunately, this approach is not moribund. There have been many recent attempts to examine the ways in which the Qur'ān and early Muslim narratives employ and think with Jewish precedents (e.g., Kugel 1990; Firestone 1990; Lassner 1993), yet many of these works can easily be overlooked because either their authors are Jewish or their works marginalized as belonging to Jewish studies. Yet all is not lost: recent years have begun to witness the re-publication of many of the works of late nineteenth-century German-Jewish scholarship (e.g., Geiger 2005; Horovitz 2002).

To return to the point with which I began this chapter, and one that I trust was not lost during the various moves made here: If a discipline is unaware of its genealogy it risks the danger of not knowing where it came from, and whence its modes of analysis derive. The work of German-Jewish scholars like Geiger must neither be ignored nor misconceived. He did not try to subvert Islam or to undermine it. On the contrary, he tried to show how Islam represented an important feature of Western civilization, a civilization that witnesses the cross-pollinization of religious ideas and categories. Certainly, we cannot simply return to Geiger's ideas and assumptions as if they were brand new, but, as I have hopefully shown, we have to acknowledge, historiographically and genealogically, his contribution to the discipline (in addition to many other scholars not mentioned here). Moreover, we have to be attuned to his major thesis that the Qur'ān is in conversation with previous terms and pericopes, and try to contextualize these historically and linguistically in the various milieux of sixth- and seventh-century Arabia.

Shaped in large part by the current political situation, as we shall see in the many of the remaining chapters, the North American study of Islam has largely moved beyond the quest for origins and gravitated towards subjects such as Sufism (Islamic mysticism) or Islam in the modern world, especially the important need to counter and dismantle forms of Islamophobia. While there is certainly nothing inherently wrong with such topics, it is worth noting that, as in all things, we do not come to "facts" objectively, but because of various institutional, political, and cultural pressures we gravitate towards certain subjects and not others. This is as true today as it was in Geiger's time. Unless we understand this, the various ways that we bring Islam into existence and/or situate it against broader geopolitical forces, the discipline risks irrelevance at best, and ossification at worst.

How we understand Islamic studies, then, must take into account the complex web of political, ideological, and social forces instrumental to the discipline's formation and current self-understanding. Unless we interrogate, in the words of J. Z. Smith, the ways we imagine religion (1982, xi), bringing it magically into existence as something distinct from other social, cultural, or rhetorical practices, we risk repeating past mistakes or accepting that which tradition has perhaps too easily forced us to accept.

2 The Invention of the Middle East: Religion and the Quest for Understanding the Muslim Mind

> Islamic Studies have always been something of a mystery to those outside the discipline. Based on the knowledge of a number of difficult languages, and focused on the examination of the historical development of a complex religion, they have assumed the character of an esoteric rite in which only a few are skilled enough to take part. They proceed according to their own, often hidden, rules; each new publication is a tactful reminder to the uninitiated that his role is to listen, to wonder, but never to question or to suggest that there might be an alternative way of doing things (Owen 1973, 287).

> The fact is that Middle Eastern studies are beset by subjective projections, displacements of affect, ideological distortion, romantic demystification, and religious bias, as well as by a great deal of incompetent scholarship (Binder 1976, 16).

The modern academic study of Islam, as I argued in the previous chapter, emerged at a particular historical moment, and out of a distinct academic trajectory, now, owing to Said's critique, pejoratively referred to as Oriental studies. The discourse used to create Islam, like those used to create other religions, was in large part imagined, manufactured, and subsequently repackaged in Europe before being imported back into the regions from which its skeletal framework had been originally extricated. The result was, as Masuzawa has demonstrated (2005), the invention of world religions, the creation of a number of global, cross-cultural objects of study, each of which was in possession of an essence regarded as not inherently different from that found in the others. More often than not, this essence was based on something internal to the individual and reflected Protestant sensibilities, such as experience over liturgy, creaturely feeling over the messiness of culture, and metaphysical beliefs over the embodiedness of ritual (see the comments in Orsi 2005, 186–92). If it were simply a matter of recognizing this oversight today all might well be fine; however, such is not the case. The repercussions of this antiquated model of an essentialized, irreducible, and *sui generis* thing called religion remains at the heart of the discipline and does not seem to be going anywhere quickly (see, e.g., the comments in Lopez 1998, 12–13). Departments of religious studies are still littered with the genealogical baggage of these constructed religions with the result that the vocabularies and categories that we employ to describe and analyze Islam (or Hinduism or Buddhism, and so on) often reveal far more about us, the creators and consumers of such vocabularies and categories, than they do about anything inherently "Islamic." To use the formulation of Daniel Dubuisson,

> The West not only conceived of the idea of religion, it has constrained other cultures to speak of their own religions by inventing them for them. Religion is not only the central concept of Western civilization, it *is* the West itself in the process of thinking the world dominated by it, by its categories of thought... Did [the discourse of religious studies] not privilege Western narcissism by allowing it to find echoes or reflections of itself everywhere? For the West's procedure has always remained the same: find its own image elsewhere, in order not to have to renounce what it thinks are universal categories...in order not to be obliged to renounce its hegemonic objectives (Dubuisson 2003, 93–94; italics in original).

If Islam was invented in the nineteenth-century German university, its imagined essence was honed and refined in the twentieth-century American academy. This move signaled an important change in emphasis. Since the study of the Orient in Europe had been, on one level, linked to the notion of empire and empire maintenance, the new gravitational pull was the Cold War, especially fears about the rise of Communism and, more specific to the newly-coined "Middle East," the production of oil. Yet, still reflecting the political and ideological concerns of a newly re-defined empire, only as Arabs and Muslims began to encroach upon American interests did they become associated with a region and the subsequent object of a new interdisciplinary program devoted to quantifying, classifying, and taxonomizing it.[1]

Whereas nineteenth-century Orientalists were primarily interested in dead Muslims accessed through a variety of classical textual traditions, American Orientalists – or, as they now preferred to call themselves, "experts in the Middle East" – tended to shift emphasis to Muslims living in the modern world. Less interested in philological skills, these social scientists (juxtaposed against what we would today call humanists) were part of a larger and optimistic *Zeitgeist* stressing interdisciplinary research in the service of a more useful and profitable form of knowledge than that traditionally produced by individual scholars working in the isolation of their offices.

The result was the invention not only of a region, the Middle East, but a scholarly program, Middle Eastern studies, to undertake the description and analysis of this imagined region (Hentsch 1992, ix–xvi). The repackaging of Oriental studies as Middle Eastern studies, the creation of a new set of emphases and methodological focuses, brought into existence a new set of data deemed worthy of analysis and quantification. Because this new area was of growing importance to public policy and provided a potential geographic check to Communism's spread, Middle Eastern studies subsequently received a good deal of governmental funding and support. This funding, unlike anything known in European universities where Orientalism began, often came from private corporations (e.g., Ford, Rockefeller) with the intention of aiding and abetting American interests. This combination of a new object of study and a governmental structure to fund it well generated considerable prestige for experts in the Middle East in the corridors of power in Washington. Yet, lurking furtively behind the formal graces and rhetorical flourishes of this new area of study resided a set of assumptions no less ideological or politicized than any produced in the previous century.

Islam, and those who considered themselves to be experts in it, played a somewhat ambiguous role in these fascinations. For the specialist in Islam was not a social scientist, but someone who was much closer to the European Orientalist of old; that is, someone interested in what we would today call humanities-based research, something not nearly as quantifiable as that done in the so-called social sciences. In order to be relevant, then, the expert in Islam had to repackage him- or herself. More often than not, as I shall argue in the second half of this chapter, this involved taking upon oneself an element of prognostication. In other words, unlike the economist, the sociologist, the political scientist, the historian, or the anthropologist, the expert in Islam claimed direct and immediate insight into the epistemic and ontological characteristics that were perceived to reside at the heart of the Middle East (now often referred to as the Islamic World), defining its essence, and thereby connecting together all the disparate cultural, historical, intellectual trajectories of the region. This discourse shared numerous operating assumptions with that produced by contemporaneous religionists; *viz.*, that the concept "religion" was somehow *sui generis*, an irreducible noumenal essence responsible for understanding other phenomena but something that could never be reduced to them. The specialist in Islam, in other words, made it his or her responsibility to articulate and explain the mental processes that created the facts that other specialists in the Middle East studied.

The Ideology of Taxonomy

Durkheim and Mauss's seminal monograph on taxonomy sheds important theoretical insight into the processes of collecting, assembling, and analyzing data. They argue that classification is neither a natural phenomenon nor does it accurately reflect the so-called natural order of things. Rather, the taxonomic act mirrors the various ways in which a particular group interacts with, and ultimately appropriates, the natural world (1969 [1903], 9). Using their claims as a point of departure, Bruce Lincoln argues that "taxonomy is hardly a neutral process, since the order established among all that is classified...is hierarchic as well as categoric" (1999, 147).

The world, in our case the Middle East, is arranged according to what is regarded as both relevant and significant to the group doing the arranging and not necessarily to that which is being arranged. The creation of scholarly conventions, often used to justify these processes, is intimately connected to this need to define a community, thereby marking its discourse off from rival discourses. As a result, those who consume information must share a similar set of cultural codes and epistemological signs with the speaker, reader, or classifier. All are caught up in a shared symbolic universe in which they buy into, are shaped by, and ultimately recapitulate the discourse that binds them. In his discussion of the ways in which discourses construct themselves and are themselves constructed, Lincoln suggests that hegemony may permutate itself in ways that those to whom we traditionally define as possessing authority might actually be little more than conduits or receptacles for those that really do:

> ...is it really the speaker who speaks to the audience...or does an audience speak to itself through the medium of the speaker? Finally, if we combine the most challenging of these possibilities (although by no means the least probable), we are led to wonder if, at least in those situations where the audience is most respectfully attentive, it might not be silencing itself in order to hear itself speak to itself through a speaker it takes to be its own representative, delegate, or incarnation? (1994, 9–10)

The various taxonomies and hierarchies inspired by these various intellectual, moral, and hegemonic concerns ultimately become, in the words of Nandy, intertwined with "a religious and ethical theory and [become] an integral part of a cosmology" (1992, 34). In many ways this process had to be (and must remain) paradoxical. On the one hand, the encounter with an imagined entity (e.g., the "Middle East") that does not literally exist apart from its proximity to America (wedged somewhere in between the "Near East" and the "Far East") forced scholars to organize and arrange the data they were trained to collect into a set of categories (e.g., political vis-à-vis economic, religious vis-à-vis secular, religious vis-à-vis cultural) mirroring their own concerns and, as Dubuisson has argued, reflecting the idiosyncratic history of the West (2003, 105). Yet, on the other hand, the encounter did not leave them (or us) unchanged because the material supplied from such encounters ultimately structured and subsequently informed the various ways in which those doing the classifying perceived, defined, and situated themselves at a particular historical moment.

The Invention of an Invention: Area Studies and the Middle East

Although area studies had preexisted the Second World War, the years 1939–1945 and those immediately afterward witnessed the creation of numerous service programs at prestigious American universities (e.g., Ivy League, Big Ten) to train individuals for jobs – intelligence, diplomatic, administrative – as quickly and as competently as possible. Of particular concern were those areas of the globe that were quickly falling within the American sphere of influence or were in danger of being subsumed by Communism (Hall 1947, 2).[2] Whereas Oriental studies, especially in places such as Germany and France, had been, in part, connected to the formation and maintenance of the colonial enterprise, the rise of area studies in America was, in many ways, a direct response to the pressures and uncertainties brought about by decolonization, and the growing strategic importance of such regions to American security and economic policy. Of especial concern, and I shall discuss this in somewhat greater detail below, was the emergence of Communism and the overwhelming fear on the part of successive American administrations that this phenomenon or worldview represented the antithesis of American political, social, and economic values. The desire to check the influence in places such as South East Asia, China, and the Middle East is inextricably linked to the creation of academic programs to study these regions.

Consequently the late 1940s witnessed the formation of such institutions as the Army Specialized Training Program (ASTP) and the Civil Affairs Training Schools (CATS) in Area and Language, both of which would prove formative in funding and developing area studies. Neither time nor space permit a detailed description of the creation and mandate of such institutions or foundations here, suffice it to say, however, that they were responsible for encouraging (and, of course, financing) American universities to train future generations of experts, both intellectual and bureaucratic, in these areas. As James B. Conant, then President of Harvard, put it:

> Among the many functions which we carried out for the armed forces during hostilities was the training of certain students sent to us by the government who

were destined to be administrators in occupied countries. A special program was constructed which included a study of the language, culture, geography, and economic background of certain countries and areas. This method of approach proved so valuable that a somewhat similar plan has now been adopted in the Graduate School of Arts and Sciences for one area, with others in prospect (quoted in Hall 1947, 18).

In order to insure that the nation would never again be found lacking in possessing a critical number of area experts, and as a means to secure such experts for the future, area studies – the interdisciplinary attempt to master the languages, culture, and economics of a particular area of the globe – came into existence. As Robert Hall, writing on behalf of the Social Science Research Council and looking into the future sustainability of area studies, understood this concept in 1947:

> There is also a national obligation which must be met if we are to live in a world of our liking. Simply to provide facts concerning places when they are needed is as yet beyond our competence. We were embarrassed during the war, when factual questions were asked. The same kind of information is needed just as much, to preserve the peace... American scholarship must penetrate and come to understand the aspirations, the traditions, the frustrations, and the many other motivations that lie behind the actions of the different peoples of the earth and give direction to their leaders. We must know, too, the broad sums of factors which make up the potentials of peoples for peaceful pursuits and war (Hall 1947, 47).

As America realized it knew very little about places that were becoming increasingly important to it, the government sought to construct institutions to manufacture and subsequently disseminate knowledge of these exotic, foreign, and strange places. Countries and regions that began to blip upon the American domestic radar automatically became the topics for such study, which in turn drove policy initiative. This knowledge – and here it is worth underscoring an important difference from that of traditional European Orientalism – was not contingent on ancient civilizations or the literary heritages that they contained, but upon the potential of their modern incarnations to rival American ascendancy and hegemony. Countries such as Russia, Japan, China, and increasingly Viet Nam became the areas of greatest concern, and the American government, through a number of agencies, was determined to make the knowledge of these places possible. The knowledge generated by such government-sponsored programs and institutions for such purposes, of course, inevitably had to be self-serving, a means to imagine, construct, and differentiate between a set of values held dear (e.g., democracy, capitalism, freedom of choice) and those deemed pernicious. All of this ultimately created a circular enterprise: Because they were potentially hostile to our interests, the objective guise of social science had to show that such regions really are different from us, that they construct and understand the world in ways that are fundamentally different from the way that we do.

The formation of such programs, however, cannot simply be reduced to practical policy initiatives. On an intellectual level, the formation of area studies was intimately connected to the rise of the projected gains associated with an interdisciplinary research agenda. Many of those involved in the formation of these new programs were certainly not aware, at least not explicitly, that their programs of research were being used in the construction of an enemy; rather, they perceived themselves to be developing academic programs and centers at the vanguard of a new method of doing research and understanding the complexity of the human condition. Those advocating the formation of such centers or programs argued that all of those interested – be they historians, economists, sociologists, or anthropologists – in a particular geographic area should pool their resources and disciplinary areas of expertise in order to be more productive in manufacturing useful, to or for whom it is never entirely clear, knowledge (Steward 1950, 2–4; Lockman 2004a, 123) than that produced using traditional disciplinary frameworks.

Of especial concern was the existence of some yet-to-be-discovered social science that would be able to uncover "universal modes" (Steward 1950, 5) of behavior, institutions and patterns occurring cross-culturally. These "universal modes," perceived to exist naturally in the world and thus simply waiting to be discovered, were made difficult to access owing to the impediments imposed by various disciplinary obstacles. Moving beyond such obstacles, it was argued that

> ascertaining universals in social science requires a definite theory and method and that, because behavior of special kinds must be understood in context as well as in isolation, the knowledge and techniques of various disciplines must be brought to bear upon these problems (Steward 1950, 6).

Area studies programs, based as they were upon interdisciplinarity and multidisciplinarity, were instrumental in such attempts to unlock this universal social science. A program devoted to, say, China could assemble a group of experts on the region, the majority of whom had received funding from the American government in order to discover and analyze the essence and *raison d'être* of this country/region. Experts on economics, sociology, political science, psychology, languages, and the religions of the area could be expected to produce a holistic knowledge of China not simply for the sake of contributing to the knowledge base of a region of the globe, but knowledge that was often framed in ways that could be reliably used for governmental consumption.

Rather than go into the ideological foundations and the administrative structures inherent to these organizations and foundations, it should suffice to examine one such institution, the Foreign Language and Area Studies Fellowship Program (otherwise known as FLAS). FLAS fellowships have been instrumental in providing American graduate students and other American academics with the requisite skills in hostile languages since the height of the Cold War. Reserved solely for American citizens and/or permanent residents, FLAS is supported by Title VI of the 1958 National Defense Education Act. For example, in the funding cycle of 2000–2002, Title VI granted the sixteen major Middle East centers a total of $2.6 million to support language and various other types of teaching, outreach, and teacher training, in addition to an additional $1.5 million in FLAS grants (Lockman 2004a, 238) to support individual language study. According to the FLAS webpage (www.ed.gov/programs/iegpsflasf/index.html), the overall goal of this program, in its various manifestations, is to

> provide academic year and summer fellowships to institutions of higher education to assist graduate students in foreign language and either area or international studies. The goals of the fellowship program include: (1) to assist in the development of knowledge, resources, and trained personnel for modern foreign language and area/international studies; (2) to stimulate the attainment of foreign language acquisition and fluency; and (3) to develop a pool of international experts to meet national needs.

FLAS, in other words, is concerned solely with the ability of American graduate students to gain expertise in a *modern* language deemed relevant to American interests. As is typical with area studies as a whole, the focus is not on classical languages to be studied for antiquarian interest, but the living, breathing languages of those regions and countries that impinge upon the national interests of the United States. For this reason one cannot receive FLAS support to study, for example, Sanskrit or classical Arabic, but one can receive such support to learn a modern Indian dialect or a regional variant of modern Arabic.

As in the previous chapter, it becomes necessary to understand our collective genealogical baggage. Here it is worthwhile to recall that before being renamed as FLAS in the 1970s, the same monies were doled out under the less innocuous National Defense Foreign Language Fellowships (NDFL). Such money, to this day, is one of the leading foundations of support for area studies programs throughout the United States. Even those who disagree with American policies in the regions they study nevertheless find it appropriate to take this money, perhaps with the understanding that it comes not directly through the CIA, but through the more innocuous channels of the Department of Education.[3]

From Oriental Studies to Middle Eastern Studies

How does the invention and subsequent study of the Middle East fit into all of this? As with the development of other regions of the globe subsumed under the category of area studies, beginning in the 1950s there existed a real concern among successive governmental administrations that the US lacked language and area experts to keep pace with American hegemony. In terms of the Arab or the Muslim World, this, as I mentioned above, directly led to the invention not only of an area, the Middle East, but also an interdisciplinary methodology, Middle Eastern studies, to describe and analyze the data produced by social-scientific experts in this region. This knowledge was maintained and funded through a variety of programs, centers, and fellowship programs established by independent foundations and later by the federal government.

The study of Islam fit problematically into Middle Eastern studies. So long as the study of Islam was concerned solely with philology and the source and redactional criticism of the Qur'ān and/or hadith, experts in the field were in danger of being classified as part of the increasingly antiquarian Oriental studies. Such knowledge could be of little use to governmental and private agencies responsible for funding areas that contributed to national interest (Kramer 2001, 11). However, once these antiquarian interests were subsumed and repackaged along the lines of a social-scientific Middle Eastern studies, whose end product would be the production and dissemination of useful knowledge, it became a perfect fit for agencies such as the Carnegie, Rockefeller, and Ford Foundations (Smock 1976, 20–22). The federal government began to add to this financial pool beginning in 1958 with grants and fellowships under Title VI of the National Defense Education Act (NDEA), at which point the knowledge of modern Arabic, Persian, and Turkish was deemed, along with many other languages, critical for the national security of the United States. According to Kramer, the results were astounding:

> In 1949, the Committee on Near Eastern Studies reported that "at no university does there appear to be a person who would claim to be an expert in the economics, sociology, or politics of present-day Near East." Twenty years later, in 1969, there were an estimated 340 full-time faculty members in Middle Eastern studies; in 1977, there were 530, and a third of them in the "hard" social sciences. In 1951, there were five Middle East programs at universities; in 1956, twelve; in 1962, eighteen; in 1970, thirty-six. In 1949, the Committee on Near Eastern Studies called for "university centers at which Near Eastern studies are more highly elaborated than elsewhere" and suggested that "three or four of these, properly spaced geographically, will suffice." In 1959, Title VI supported three Middle East Centers; in 1964, eight; in 1970, fifteen (Kramer 2001, 12).[4]

This growth in the academic study of Islam and the Near East is highly significant and cannot simply be reduced to a scholarly interest in these areas. There can be no coincidence, for example, that as the CIA was helping to organize a military coup in Iran in 1953 to install the Shah, funding to establish a knowledge base of this region was trebling at American universities. The increasing encroachment of the Middle East on American national interests was thus directly responsible for the rise in the discovery of data deemed significant to national and economic welfare. Within this context, area studies portrayed itself as the best way to uncover and interpret this data (see Lockman 2004a, 123). These programs prided themselves on their interdisciplinary and multidisciplinary approach to a single region. Only such an approach, a 1948 Social Science Reseach Council report, argued, "is capable of dealing with the complexities of the culture and environment of an area. The geographic limits of an area induce the specialists to pool their knowledge and prevent them from ignoring the relevance of factors which are outside the domains habitually considered by any one of them" (quoted in Wallerstein 1997, 205).

Islamic Motivations

The interdisciplinary nature of area studies was but one attempt to overcome disciplinary allegiance in the grand service of developing precisely such a universal social science. In the case of the Middle East (with the obvious exception of Israel), a decontextualized, ahistorical phenomenon called "Islam" was invented to try and explain why people in this region think the way they do. In other words, how and why did Islam motivate people to think or act in a certain way, to make certain choices, and to imagine the world in a particular way as opposed to others. This neatly-packaged and monolithic Islam was, in turn, constructed as a distinct system that could be neatly distinguishable from and irreducible to other cultural, social, or economic forms. Although the study of Islam has today largely migrated out of Middle Eastern studies into the murky realm of religious studies, we are still often left with the vestigial remnants of this monolithic Islam. In fact, as I shall argue in the following chapter, it is a discourse that Islamicists inherited directly and consciously from religious studies. For example, it is this essential Islam that we invoke whenever we talk about the "five pillars," the prohibitions against alcohol and pork, the extreme version of monotheism (*tawhīd*), or an equally reified non-violent Islam. This neatly constructed Islam masks, of course, the various ways that some set of objects and/or ideologies known collectively as "Islam" is appealed to in order to justify the political and authoritative claims that various groups, vying with one another, make in order to define and reproduce themselves.

"Islam" qua religion poses a problem to Middle Eastern studies. Since the study of religion is traditionally marginal to the social sciences (e.g., sociology, political science), experts in the religion of Islam had to redefine their specialty. Islam now became the key to understanding the thought processes or motivations of individuals, groups, or even whole regions. It is this rather vague and amorphous claim that still haunts Islamicists (e.g., "Islam doesn't...," "Muslims claim..."). The idea that religion somehow provides useful insight into the ontological processes and inner motivations of a people or nation is predicated on a discourse claiming that since religion emerges from a numinous experience with something transcendent, such an experience must therefore illumine the essence of a group. The study of such experiences, as the likes of Fitzgerald (2000) and McCutcheon (1997, 2003) have well argued, is subsequently claimed to be the *raison d'être* of the professional religionist. Based on his or her professional expertise with the "numinous" or the "sacred," the scholar of religion claims to have a unique vantage point from which to witness the generation or establishment of beliefs, practices, and social structures. According to this model, religion is a phenomenon that is always taken for granted as that which informs other cultural or ideological practices, but is something that is never informed or, heaven forbid, created by such practices.

To cite one example of this model of how religion is used and abused, let me examine briefly a conference, sponsored by the Ford Foundation, and held in Belgium during September 1953. Convened by the great Islamicist, and subsequent head of Middle Eastern studies at UCLA, Gustav von Grunebaum (1909–1972),[5] the problem that this conference sought to examine was the role of "Unity and Diversity in Muslim Civilization." As Jacques Duchesne-Guillemin wrote in his preface to the collection of edited papers, the practical goal that these Middle Eastern experts sought to ascertain, the problem they desired to solve, was how Islam might play a leading role in the solidarity and modernization of Islamic countries:

> We are led then, if we are at all concerned with the defense of Suez, the relations between Israel and her neighbors, Moroccan autonomy, the independence of Persia or of Pakistan, and the resistance of all these regions to external and internal Communist danger, to wonder what in our day can still be involved in the fact of being Muslim, which is potentially the basis of a confederation of which the Arab league is only a dream (Duchesne-Guillemin 1955, 3).

From this quotation we can conveniently catch a glimpse of a number of factors responsible for the situation of Islam in the aftermath of the Second World War and at the height of the Cold War. "The disorder and poverty which rage in the Middle East" (Duchesne-Guillemin 1955, 3) posed a serious threat to stability in the region. The potential nefarious influence of Communism, including its role in the increasing tensions between the Palestinians and the Israelis, threatened to undermine the American sphere of influence. To remedy the situation, the Ford Foundation funded a series of conferences and workshops, of which *Unity and Variety in Muslim Civilization* was but one, in order to assess the risk, and ultimately to help formulate governmental policy.[6]

Von Grunebaum, responsible for convening the conference, claims as his contribution the rather huge task of understanding how and why Muslims think the way they do. In other words, his area of expertise is a unique insight into the Islamic *Weltanschauung* writ large. For him, the academic study of Islam enables us to examine the Muslim psyche, providing real insights into why Muslims (both individually and collectively) make the choices they do:

> So the achievement of Islām in transforming the ancestral Arab culture may be presented as the introducing of four fundamental changes: (a) a widening and refinement of human sensibilities; b) an extension of the intellectual world and of the means of its mastery by man; (c) the creation of a morally justified and at the same time effective political organization of a locally unprecedented structure; and (d) the delineation of a new "standard" type of life, that is, a new human ideal, and a detailed pattern for its realization in a model biography extending from conception to beyond the day of judgment (1955, 22).

The operating assumption here is that religion functions as an epistemological canopy, that all who exist under it must see the world in the same way and possess the same motivations. This, of course, is a difficult if not impossible case to make. How can religion, itself a product of various cultural and ideological constructions, be able to circle back, shed light on, and subsequently be described as that which creates human thought and culture in the first place? Von Grunebaum, like so many of those who specialized in the religion of Islam in Middle Eastern studies programs, gave religion far too much credit in human conduct as a way to carve out areas of expertise for themselves, so that they would not be left behind as the social-scientific paradigm dominated the field of Middle Eastern studies. If one could claim such expertise in the very thought processes of a group, then naturally all of the other disciplinary experts in Middle Eastern studies programs would be seen as dependent on the expert in Islam. This is certainly not to say that such scholars did not make important contributions to our understanding of *certain features* of the

2 The Invention of the Middle East

area or that they worked with grossly misguided models. However, we do need to remind ourselves that much like the Orientalists of the nineteenth century and no different than us today, these Middle Eastern experts in Islam were the product of political, ideological, and social contexts that helped to construct the way they thought about and subsequently situated Islam. Indeed, it could not be otherwise as I am trying to argue here, because scholars of Islam must imagine Islam in their own images and these images are always situated in social contest and construction.

Another contributor to the volume was (and still remains) the controversial Bernard Lewis. Lewis, whose topic at the seminar was "Turkey: Westernization," argued that what made the Turks unique in their embrace of Europe was their different encounter with Islam:

> The Islām of the Turkish frontiersmen was thus of a different quality from that of the heartlands of Islām. Unlike their brothers who had gone to Iraq or Egypt as Mamlūks and been brought up in the very different atmosphere of the old Islamic capitals, the free Turks were Islamized and educated in the borderlands, and their Islām was from the first impregnated with the special characteristics of the frontier. Their teachers were dervishes, wandering monks, and mystics, usually Turkish, preaching a very different faith from that of the theologians and the seminaries of the cities (Lewis 1955, 323).

Common to this seminar, then, was the notion that Islam was a unified semantic field responsible for motivating people to act, deterministically, in a certain manner. And, as Lewis's contribution argues, when Muslims do act differently it has very little to do with a secular dictator such as Ataturk, but must be the result of the "frontier" Islam that the Turks encountered centuries ago.

Although of late Bernard Lewis has been interested in the various civilizational impediments between "Islam" and "modernity" (2003), he was not always interested in this topic. In the mid-1950s, at the height of the Cold War, for instance, his main interest was in "Islam" and "Communism":

> In the present competition between Western democracies and Soviet Communism for the support of the Islamic world, what factors or questions are there in Islamic tradition, or in the present state of Islamic society and opinion, which might prepare intellectually and politically active groups to embrace Communist principles and methods of governments, and the rest to accept them? (1954, 1)

Here, once again, Lewis assumes that there exists some kind of Islamic mentality that motivates Muslims, *en masse*, to gravitate (or not) towards certain principles, be it Communism then or Modernity now.[7] For Lewis, the "Islamic" social order, again something constructed in monolithic terms, predetermines Muslims to think and behave in certain ways. In the following passage, Lewis links these ways to the agricultural cycle of the Middle East:

> The classical Islamic social order was evolved in Iraq and Egypt, and confined to the ancient pattern of river valley society. In those lands of little rainfall there was an intensive agriculture, based on artificial irrigation from the river... For this system a strong central authority was a paramount necessity, and one does not have to look far to find examples of the ruin and impoverishment which followed the breakdown of the central authority in times of political weakness and the consequent neglect of the irrigation works (1954, 9).

The figure of H. A. R. Gibb (1895–1971) further attests to the self-importance of the specialist in Islam in the emerging interdisciplinary programs of Middle Eastern studies. Gibb was a faculty member in Oriental studies at the University of Oxford before taking up a position at Harvard in 1955. His move was directly connected to the increased funding that area studies in general and Middle Eastern studies in particular was then receiving at American universities. At Harvard, for instance, Gibb became the founding director of the newly established Center for Middle Eastern Studies. He also became part of the new SSRC-ACLES Joint Committee on the Near and Middle East, whose goal was "to promote and guide the development of Middle East Studies in the United States" (Lockman 2004a, 127). Gibb, to protect and justify his own training in the field, was adamant that the study of the Middle East not exclude those who studied Islam (using the parlance of the time, he refers to these people as "Orientalists"). For only such an individual possessed the unique ability to

> bring together and correlate the findings of the separate social studies... The Orientalist's function is to furnish that [central] core out of his knowledge and understanding of the invisibles – the values, attitudes and mental processes characteristic of the "great culture" that underlie the application even today of the social and economic data – to explain the why, rather than the what and the how, and this precisely because he is or should be able to see the data not simply as isolated facts, explicable in and by themselves, but in the broad context and long perspective of cultural habit and tradition (quoted in Lockman 2004a, 130).

This assumption that the Islamicist, based on the expertise that he or she has acquired during graduate school or extensive travel in the region, possess some innate ability to grasp and apprehend something as intangible as religion is certainly a problematic claim, and one that is still often appealed to by Islamicists in religious studies departments to this day. Explicit in Gibb's comments is that the Islamicist/Orientalist is able to understand a phenomenon pre-defined in advance as Islam, something generally acknowledged to be one of several "world religions." This, in

2 The Invention of the Middle East

turn, permits such an expert to comprehend the thought processes and the social structures of a particular region of the globe. As Gibb argues in this passage, the Islamicist/Orientalist (we can also read here religionist) has a distinct function to contribute to the interdisciplinary study of a region. Whereas others may study the economy of, say, Egypt, the political system of Turkey, the social makeup of a particular village in Morocco, the Islamicist alone is able to ground all of these processes in a particular, and presumably universal, Islamic *Weltanschauung*. Writing in another context, Gibb argues that

> what is so difficult for the Western student to grasp [is] the aversion of the Muslims from the thought-processes of rationalism. [The defeat of rationalist schools of thought in the early centuries of Islam] not only conditioned the formulation of the traditional Muslim theology but set a permanent stamp upon Islamic culture; and they still lie behind the conflicts arising in more recent years out of direct contact with modern Western thought. The rejection of rationalist modes of thought and of the utilitarian ethic which is inseparable from them has its roots, therefore, not in the so-called "obscurantism" of the Muslim theologians but in the atomism and discreteness of the Arab imagination (1972 [1947], 5, 7; quoted in Lockman 2004a, 108–109).

For Gibb, according to this passage, the Islamicist or Orientalist possesses insight into the Arab mind and his or her "imagination." Grounding this mind or imagination in the classical sources of Islam (e.g., the conflict over Islamic orthodoxy as it emerged out of the competing schools of theology in classical Islam) is the *raison d'être* of this specialist. The ability to move effortlessly between classical Islamic history and the contemporary Arab mind, in other words, is the self-perceived specialty of the individual who works on the religion of Islam.

Much of Gibb's claims, like those of others in the study of religion,[8] mirror the desire of professional religionists to secure not only administrative space for themselves, but also some unique insight into human behavior. By claiming that they are the sole interpreters of religion and/or the religious, Gibb and others define and subsequently protect an ill-defined and autonomous data and methodology that they alone are uniquely qualified to study and administer. This assumption that one can study humans as if disembodied intellects that are somehow divorced from various cultured, gendered, economic, political, and ideological categories is one of the hallmarks not only of the way Islam has been studied in Middle Eastern studies, but also of the modern academic study of religion.

If Islamic studies has, as the previous chapter showed, one foot in the antiquarian fields of nineteenth-century Europe, the invention of the

"Middle East" and the inter-disciplinary framework to study it – so-called "Middle Eastern studies" – has a distinctly twentieth-century and American provenance. The various founders of Middle Eastern studies were quick to differentiate their topic of concern from their genealogical antecedents of Oriental studies. In particular, the study of the Arab or Middle Eastern epistemes or mentalities moved out of the arena of philology and history – although a practical knowledge of both would still remain necessary – into the arena of political science, sociology, and economics. The shift in emphasis moved the study of the Orient out of the humanities into the social sciences, where it became reinvented as "Middle Eastern studies." This created a disciplinary backlash against studying classical texts simply for their own sake. However, as I tried to argue in this chapter, some now perceived such texts as contributing to the ongoing taxonomizing and categorization of the region because they illumined how people in the Middle East think today. This would produce its own backlash in the form of Islamic studies, the subject of the following chapter, an attempt by some to return to the humanistic study of Islamic texts.

3 Tensions Past, Tensions Future: Middle Eastern Studies Confronts Religious Studies

> That is to say, while there is a staggering amount of data, of phenomena, of human experiences and expressions that might be characterized in one culture or another, by one criterion or another, as religious – *there is no data for religion*. Religion is solely the creation of the scholar's study. It is created for the scholar's analytic purposes by his imaginative acts of comparison and generalization. Religion has no independent existence apart from the academy. For this reason, the student of religion, and most particularly the historian of religion, must be relentlessly self-conscious. Indeed, this self-consciousness constitutes his primary expertise, his foremost object of study (J. Z. Smith 1982, xi; original italics).

The 1970s saw the academy increasingly turn its attention away from attempts to discover a set of illusory and illusive "universal modes" of human behavior. Universalism subsequently came under attack from various constituencies as little more than another form of political and ideological hegemony, the will to power of a dominant group over others. This shift in emphasis, driven in large part by postmodern critiques of the Enlightenment project, questioned many of the operating assumptions that were traditionally assumed as *de riguer*, including traditional binary oppositions such as center/margin, male/female, white/non-white, and the interpretive strategies that tended to privilege the first term of each of these constructs at the expense of the second. This critique was intimately connected to the politics of representation and the concomitant desire to subvert traditional types of knowledge production. What epistemological assumptions, for example, supported and legitimated traditional forms of knowing? How did disciplinary boundaries protect these forms, marginalizing all that did not fit neatly within their parameters? Could these disciplinary boundaries be expanded to include other groups and ethnicities in such a manner that did not privilege the dominant hegemonic structures of the West?

The critique of the Enlightenment project had massive repercussions, in many ways permanently de-centering traditional canons and truth claims of university disciplines. These traditional canons and claims, it was argued, did not so much accurately describe the world observed from some Archimedean fulcrum point as mirror the concerns, obsessions, and fantasies of those doing the observation. The perceived clear and transcendental gaze of the researcher was undermined and gave way to perspectival encounters based upon more quotidian features such as race, gender, ethnicity, and socio-economic class. Increasingly the traditionally marginalized and occluded began to poke holes at what they considered to be the false claims of stability and perpetuity of knowledge production. Feminism, Black studies, Chicano studies, Jewish studies, etc. now all argued for the inclusion of different kinds of knowledge based upon their own experiences, all the while showing that traditional forms of disciplinary self-understanding were neither as objective nor as value-neutral as claimed (Juschka 2006, 391–92). At the same time, however, in challenging such disciplinary boundaries, knowledge generated by and about those others (marked by class, race, geo-political location and/or gender) was considered to be of marginal value or to be partisan and therefore inadequate as defined by and within so-called "legitimate" disciplines (Juschka 2006, 395–98).

These trajectories of politics, identity, and inclusion would play a large role in situating Islam beginning in the 1970s. Although I shall examine the politics of identity in greater detail in the following chapter, I here focus on the difficult and still ongoing migration of the study of Islam out of Middle Eastern studies and into departments of religious studies. I frame this migration against the perceived excesses of philological skills associated with Orientalism, and the increased need to take refuge from these excesses in the inner experiences, often amorphously associated with faith claims, of those studied. The academic study of religion, especially its claims of ineffability and the *sui generis* nature of religious belief as articulated in the 1960s and 1970s, provided a useful refuge for those migrating out of area studies. Such claims, according to Rosalind Shaw, had the advantage of insulating scholars of religion in general, and I would add scholars of Islam in particular, from asking (and answering) various uncomfortable questions (1995, 70).

In order to elucidate these claims, the present chapter examines several key thinkers that I deem responsible, in various ways, for orientating the study of Islam in the direction of religious studies. These individuals – Wilfred Cantwell Smith, Marshal G. S. Hodgson, and Fazlur Rahman – saw faith and experience (or "conscience" in Hodgson's parlance) as irreducible factors internal to individuals. Such *internal* experiences were, in turn, perceived as somehow responsible for the creation of various *external* cultural and social manifestations. Although all three of these scholars provided useful critiques of traditional Orientalist scholarship, all ultimately, albeit for different reasons, had no choice but to argue for a universal set of Islamic faith experiences responsible for guiding and shaping Islam in and through various temporal and geographical contexts.

Before I examine these figures in greater detail, however, I provide a brief analysis of the impact that the politics of representation and representation of politics has had on the academic study of Islam. My argument here is that the unpopularity of the Cold War (culminating in Viet Nam), the Foucauldian elements inherent to Said's critique, and the desire of minorities (and those sympathetic to them) to represent themselves has produced a reified Islam no less situated than that produced by Orientalists or practitioners of area studies. Indeed, it is as pernicious precisely because it was forced to fall back upon experiential claims that are internal to individuals and that cannot be subject to social-scientific critique.

Area Studies and the Turn Towards the Politics of Representation

The 1960s and 1970s gave birth to a generation raised on the excesses of the Viet Nam War and the increasing dissatisfaction with tradition and its various modes of hegemony. Whereas area studies of the years immediately following the Second World War had been interested in working with the American government in the pursuit of public policy initiatives, the late 1960s and 1970s increasingly witnessed a critique of such policy and a growing awareness of the colonialist ills perpetuated against the so-called Third World. If the area studies of the 1940s and 50s had prided themselves on their optimism and their desire to uncover the "universal modes" of humanity, the following decades witnessed the growing realization of the subjectivity of the researcher, the relativity of knowledge, and the gradual uneasiness associated with working in collusion with a superpower, one whose political aims were often at odds with the values that one studied and with which one often identified.

An important cog in this wheel of de-legitimizing traditional disciplinary conventions and its claims to possessing universal canons of scholarship was the publication in 1978 of Said's *Orientalism*. This work, one upon which I have either commented or will comment in every chapter of this study, has had, I am suggesting, an extremely problematic impact on the field of Islamic studies. As I have tried to argue, however, it is only by reassessing this work's claims, examining its reception history, and contextualizing its political and ideological implications that we can, hopefully, move forward.

In terms of the present context, Said's claim that all knowledge of the East, the so-called "Orient," was invested in political and ideological domination struck a chord with American intellectuals who were at this time not only growing extremely critical of American foreign policy, but also just encountering for the first time in English translation the work of Michel Foucault and other French theorists critical of the status quo. As a result, the claim that all scholarship (not to mention art, music, and literature) produced in the West by non-Easterners was somehow connected to Western domination and imperialism (Said 1993, 3–14) convinced many American academics. It was probably no coincidence that this also coincided with the aftermath of the Vietnam War and American involvement in Lebanon and Iran.

All of these factors led to a growing realization that knowledge was not neutral, but could be and was often used in the oddest of ways to justify and legitimate certain truth claims. This led to the awareness of the intersection between political and intellectual agendas. Of especial relevance was the question of identity and the ability to speak on behalf of others. Who, in other words, should be allowed to represent others? What are the epistemological and ontological categories that make such representation possible? Why should people outside of a particular group or at least unsympathetic to them be allowed to have the final say in representation?

As the politics of identity increased, minorities, long marginalized if not left completely out of the ranks of the professorate, increasingly sought out their place in the Academy. Such groups believed, correctly or incorrectly is not my concern here, that they had something to contribute to the ongoing attempts at taxonomizing, representing, and understanding those regions of the globe from which they came. The only problem, as we shall shortly see, is that in order to contribute to the emerging discourse on such regions and areas, these groups not only had to employ the same categories as those they criticized, even more problematically such groups increasingly relied on and appealed to the rather amorphous qualities associated with "experience" in order to validate their epistemological and ontological claims.

In disciplines dealing with the Middle East and Islam, this reaction against Orientalism and the ills of colonialism and imperialism led to more calls for Arabs and Muslims to enter the ranks of graduate schools and increasingly the professorate. Using Said's critique of the discipline's genealogy, it was easy to argue that the academic study of the Islamic world and the Middle East had always fallen within the purview of white European males. As a result, it was argued that minorities from Middle Eastern and Muslim backgrounds, or perhaps even those Caucasian Americans who had converted to Islam or at least were sympathetic to its teachings,

3 Tensions Past, Tensions Future

should now be allowed to represent themselves, their cultures real or imagined, and their religious traditions.

This desire to represent oneself tended to coincide, at least in circles that rub up against religion, with the politics of nostalgia and the quest for authenticity. The construction of identity – national, religious, or otherwise – does not simply arise ex nihilo, however, but is something that is actively constructed and contested over time (Eagleton 1991, 45–51). Looking back at this construction it is all too easy to appeal to the notion that it was an organic process, based on unified notions of language, culture, ethnicity, religion, etc. According to Aijaz Ahmad, however, the results of such a nostalgia should not be all that surprising given the class, gender, and level of education of these individuals:

> Its most passionate following in the metropolitan countries is within those sectors of the university intelligentsia which either originate in the ethnic minorities or affiliate themselves ideologically with the academic sections of those minorities... These [immigrants] who came as graduate students and then joined the faculties, especially in the Humanities and Social Sciences, tended to come from upper classes in their home countries. In the process of relocating themselves in the metropolitan countries they needed documents of their assertion, proof that they had always been oppressed... What the upwardly mobile professionals in this new immigration needed were narratives of oppression that would get them preferential treatment, reserved jobs, higher salaries in the social position they already occupied: namely as middle-class professionals, mostly male. For such purposes *Orientalism* was the perfect answer (Ahmad 1992, 195–96).

The politics of identity and the tendency towards self-representation on the part of "native" scholars has created another set of imaginings and perceived essences. These new representations, much like their predecessors, were based on a distinct epistemology grounded in an ontology of what it means to be colonized and represented by others. As a result, only those who were part of a particular religion or from a specific ethnic group or those sufficiently sympathetic to the deleterious effects of colonialism, American imperialism or Israeli aggression were allowed to define the parameters of definition and representation. Being of a particular religion or of a particular ethnicity, in other words, provided a perceived vantage point, albeit one often as problematically constructed as that of the Orientalists, from which to make claims that were (and still are) often as unfounded as those produced by those they criticized as biased or based on unfounded presuppositions.

If the specialist on Islam in Middle Eastern studies programs was able to claim an expertise based on his or her ability to read classical texts and infer from them something of modern Muslim thought processes, then the person who now identified with his or her data through religious or ethnic affiliation could do something similar based on genetics. It is precisely this tension of representation – who can or should be allowed to represent others? What are the consequences of such representation? – that resides at the heart of any humanistic study, especially that which is normatively though not unproblematically referred to as religion. In studying Islam, however, there is the even thornier question of dealing with a set of traditions that have historically and theologically been constructed as a hostile other.

Nowhere is this more in evidence than in the current post-9/11 moment when many who study Islam professionally feel compelled to speak out publicly on behalf of Muslims to defend them of the various charges leveled against them. In itself, there is nothing inherently wrong with defending those who have been wrongly accused or who are deemed guilty by association. This is not the point. What is at issue for the academic study of Islam, I submit, is the tone and assumptions that underlie these defenses. More often than not, and I shall discuss this in greater detail in Chapter 5, this defense pivots on the claim that Islam somehow possesses a stable essence to which Muslims simply and passively assent. This essence is then held up as "good" or as "authentic" and all that departs from it as being somehow "heterodox" or as just plain "wrong."

Although this topic will concern me in the remaining chapters of this study, let it suffice here to state that a close identification with our objects of study, the need to defend them in the media, to speak for them at churches or synagogues, to represent them at inter-faith dialogues, cannot nor should not be part of the religionist's conceptual apparatus. This phenomenon, which I am here intimating emerges out of the Saidian critique of the discipline, is having a deleterious effect as scholars of Islam continually blur the line between critic and caretaker, outsider and insider.

Neither the Orientalist nor the apologist approach – to remove them briefly from their genealogical baggage let me re-label them here as the epistemological and the genetic – provides a proper understanding of something called Islam precisely because no such thing can exist. Despite appeals to the contrary by either practitioners or scholars of the tradition, Islam, like any other religious tradition, is a series of sites of contestation, where regimes of perceived truth do battle against other such regimes in the service of something murkily called authority, tradition, or authenticity. These series of overlapping contestations, the need to legitimate an in-group, are by no means static or stable, nor are they entirely transparent to the researcher's gaze. Any attempt to arrive at a uniform or authentic experience, even if such an experience could be agreed upon by consensus, I submit, is purely a chimera driven by all sorts of extra-intellectual agendas.

Despite calls to the contrary, the epistemological and the genetic approaches to Islamic data share many homologous features. For instance, both are concerned, albeit for different reasons, with uncovering or recovering some authentic experience at a particular moment in time. Why this should be the case is unclear, but more than likely it has to do with ascertaining some normative or orthodox version of the tradition with which to measure later or contemporaneous heterodoxies. The best example from recent years is the hijackers of 9/11 and the broader al-Qaeda network. How does one understand groups such as these? If they can be circumscribed as either "bastardizers" of a normative Islam or as not even Muslim (e.g., Nasr 2002; Armstrong 2000; 2001, Esposito 2003), then it becomes all too easy, with a series of neat rhetorical moves, to circumscribe such individuals and groups beyond the pale of Islam and thus beyond a particular mode of analysis. (Of course, the opposite approach – to view such groups as normative Islam – is equally pernicious, and leads to just as many fallacious conclusions.)

Moreover, and as if this were not problematic enough, such an act of extrication is contingent upon a perceived set of experiences deemed authentic. These experiences are subsequently labeled "universal" and then neatly applied to other spatial and temporal periods in something that is problematically labeled as "Islamic civilization." This manufacturing and subsequent dissemination of normativity erases the messiness and contradictions of what goes into the formation of group identity, marginalizing the problematic, the totalitarian – in other words, all that upsets us.

Finally, the rhetoric of tradition and authenticity forces scholars of Islam to accept as given those constructions that we like, and to dismiss as biased those with which we disagree (whether historical or academic). The result is that our own rhetoric of academic tradition and authenticity has prevented us from moving far beyond various normative discussions. The best evidence for this is, once again, the aftermath of 9/11. The most interesting discussions of this event came not from experts in Islam, many of whom appealed to the orthodox/heterodox, authentic/inauthentic, real/false, and essence/margin dichotomies (e.g., Armstrong 2000, 2001; Esposito 1999 [1992], 2003, 2005 [1988]; Geertz 2003b; Levine 2005; Nasr 2002), but from those completely outside the discipline (e.g., Lincoln 2003; McCutcheon 2005; Orsi 2005) who were willing to connect such events to a critical apparatus supplied by a specific discourse in the academic study of religion, one that refuses to submit to the claims of believers and that is unwilling to rely on claims to some ambiguous, and thus unanalyzable, set or sets of inner experiences.

Back to Basics

The point to make here, if it is not painfully obvious, is that any attempt to define Islam or the Middle East is bound to fail for at least two reasons. First, the person doing the interpreting – whether a Middle East expert talking about the way Muslims think or a Muslim academic claiming to speak for a civilization – is always situated and their research is always guided by genealogies that determine the questions asked and the answers deemed satisfactory. It is quite impossible to assume that objective reconstruction, analysis, or description exists in our constant endeavor to engage with human civilizations. Sub-textual and extra-textual interests drive research; without them we would never have the initiative to approach data in the first place. Yet, and this is why I use the quotation from Smith to open this chapter, we must constantly be aware of and self-reflexive of why we approach data in the first place and why we are drawn to certain questions. There is certainly nothing fundamentally wrong with either non-Muslims or Muslims studying Islam. In fact, the latter category makes much sense given the fact that many Muslims are interested in the textual, cultural, historical, intellectual, and religious dimensions of something that is often rather lazily dubbed as Islam. However, this interest cannot be replaced by appeals to personal insight, claims to a transcendental order, or claims to some form of idiosyncratic or anecdotal data not available to others. Such a hermeneutic, long used to justify the professional religionist's area of expertise, does not represent valid academic criteria for the study of Islam, or any other religious tradition (see the comments in Arnal 2005, 73–74). To use the words of Bruce Lincoln:

> I not only grant but insist that scholarship – like human speech in general – is interested, perspectival, and partial and that its ideological dimensions must be acknowledged, ferreted out where necessary and critically cross-examined (1999, 208).

With this statement, Lincoln goes on to argue that scholarship must nevertheless proceed cautiously, constantly be on guard that its *mythoi* are not assumed to be part of the natural order and that its mythopoesis not be mistaken for objective narratives. Scholarship, in other words, must be understood to be "myth with footnotes":

Ideally, footnotes mark the fact that a scholarly text is not a discourse of free inventions, wherein ideological interests escape all controls. Rather, they serve as a visible reminder that scholarly texts result from a dialectic encounter between an interested inquirer, a body of evidence, and a community of other competent and interested researchers, past, present, and future. *All who participate are committed to a sustained engagement with the data and also with one another, their engagement being mediated by shared principles of theory and method, which – like the evidence and its interpretation – are subject to renegotiation in the space of their texts and their conversations* (Lincoln 1999, 208; my italics).

Precisely because such attempts to understand must always be situated, the study of ancient texts or a genetic affiliation with the material that one studies can provide no objective insight into a particular religion. Identity is not neatly inscribed, as people assent to or dissent from a set of texts deemed canonical by experts; neither can the existence of such an identity, to use the words of McCutcheon, "rely on an ahistorical view of the past as a linear and uniform medium in which pristine meanings are communicated from an originary moment to the present" (2005, 60). On the contrary, identity, whether of the personal or group variety, is fraught with manifold ruptures and fissures, which are often bridged or filled by appeals to various political, ideological, taxonomical, and rhetorical devices that all too often masquerade as some normative religious affiliation. Our mistake, *qua* scholars, is to paint over all of these constructions with the rather insipid phrase "religion" (or, in the present case, "Islam") as if it provided a unitary set of meanings that are easily and readily accessible.

Our job in the academic study of Islam must be to examine not that people and groups, historically and in the present, call themselves Muslims or make appeals to something nebulously called Islam, but why they do so and how they go about this. What rhetorical moves do such individuals and collectivities make? What informs such moves, and makes their ends desirable or not? How is tradition actively constructed? What are the external forces that lead to the creation, and subsequent maintenance, of something that is later referred to as authentic?

The academic study of Islam has, according to my arguments in this study, veered drastically off course. Rather than providing a set of understandings of how Muslims contest and construct identity, there is a tendency to accept such construction as essential. This lack of focus, as I shall argue in the rest of this chapter, is connected to a particular discourse that Islamicists inherited from the academic study of religion during the 1960s and 1970s. These years witnessed the rise of the *sui generis* discourse in religious studies and the concomitant notion that religion was something irreducible and part and parcel of inner experience as opposed to something embedded in various historical, social, and ideological contexts. This discourse entered into the academic study of Islam at a particular moment and in response to a number of external forces. Despite the mounting criticism of the *sui generis* ideology in certain circles associated with theory and method in the academic study of religion today, it unfortunately remains virtually unassailable in the study of Islam.

Wilfred Cantwell Smith's Integrative Paradigm

An instrumental figure in attempting to secure a place for Islam within the comparative religion model that was popular in the years following World War Two was the Canadian Wilfred Cantwell Smith (1916–2001). Trained at the University of Cambridge, Cantwell Smith spent the years 1940–1945 in India, where he taught Islamic and Indian History at the Forman Christian College in Lahore. There he was engaged in facilitating, among other things, Muslim-Hindu dialogue in the years immediately preceding partition (Putnam et al. 2001; Cracknall 2001, 5–6). In 1949 Cantwell Smith was appointed the Birks Professor of Comparative Religion at McGill University in Montreal, and in 1951 at the same institution he became the founding director of the Institute of Islamic Studies. His goal in founding this Institute at McGill was, in the words of its librarian, to

> understand and interpret the Muslim faith and the Islamic tradition…[in] an essentially co-operative enterprise undertaken jointly by Muslims and Westerners. The global quality of the study is also enhanced by the participation of some scholars who are neither Muslim nor Western. Insofar as it is feasible, the teaching and research staff and also the student body numbers are approximately half Muslim and half Western… The Institute endeavors to offer to Westerners a serious encounter with a civilization other than their own. It recognizes that such an experience, in order to be valid, may require a creative modification of one's own terms of reference. It strives to help Western students understand and appreciate an important, rich and varied civilization. To Muslims, the Institute aspires to offer an opportunity to study their own society in a serious, disciplined, scientific, and sympathetic environment, and to understand the international setting in which their society is currently involved and the problems that in modern times their faith must face. The Institute was founded for the purpose of engaging in the serious study of the modern Muslim world. The innovative element was Smith's conviction that this could not be done effectively by non-Muslims studying in a non-Muslim institution and without the participation of Muslims. The design for the Institute, including the design for the library, was the result of his creative response to the dilemma, as he saw it, of how to study Islam in a way that would involve Muslims and non-Muslims (Ferahian 2001).

3 Tensions Past, Tensions Future

Cantwell Smith thus hoped to facilitate a dialogue between Muslims and non-Muslims in a collective enterprise. His model behind this dialogue may well have been his experiences in seeing Muslims and Hindus talk together in India under his auspices at the Forman Christian College. Like the Middle Eastern studies programs then in vogue, Cantwell Smith brought together under one administrative canopy a number of scholars from different disciplines. Unlike the Middle Eastern studies programs, however, the Institute was a *humanistic* endeavor to understand the religion of Islam broadly conceived as a trans-regional civilization as opposed to a particular geographic region from a social-scientific perspective. Smith's other goal in forming the Institute was to have a center in which there would exist an equal number of Muslim and non-Muslim students and faculty who would undertake collaborative study of the Islamic world, writ large (Cracknell 2001, 7).

In 1964 Cantwell Smith was appointed as a professor at Harvard University, where he succeeded Robert Slater, who had been the founding director of the Center for the Study of World Religions. In the late 1970s, as Director of the Center, Cantwell Smith was instrumental in making sure that all graduate students engage in "comparative" research at the doctoral level. Here, it is perhaps worthwhile to understand what the term comparison, always a thorny one even at the best of times, meant to Cantwell Smith. To use his own words:

> ...a statement about religion, in order to be valid, must be intelligible and acceptable to those within. In order to be sincere and of any use, it must also of course be intelligible and acceptable to the outsider who makes it. When Muslims and Buddhists meet, what is needed are a statement of Islam that Muslims can recognize as valid and Buddhists can recognize as meaningful, and similarly a statement about Buddhism that Buddhists can acknowledge and Muslims understand... This can be generalized so that herein is posed one of the fundamental tasks of our studies today. I would formulate it thus: *it is the business of comparative religion to construct statements about religion that are intelligible within at least two traditions simultaneously*. This is not easy, it has not been done systematically in the past and almost not done at all; but it is intellectually important and historically urgent (W. C. Smith 1959, 52; his italics).

Cantwell Smith undoubtedly had many altruistic reasons to engage in something known as the "comparative study of religion," such as the noble vision of creating a set of ecumenical preconditions in which various religions could speak to one another. But how does the scholar of religion fit into this overtly liberal Protestant theological program? If our work is circumscribed to re-telling and re-packaging for the consumption of, simultaneously, the people we study and our local clergy, we might well succeed in getting Christians and Muslims talking to one another, but how does this make us understand any better the messy business of religion and the manifold ways various groups appeal to it for legitimation? Religion, according to this model, is not something that is constructed and appealed to by various historical agents, but a stable essence based on how devotees understand and interpret to themselves what it is they do or think they do.

Cantwell Smith works on the assumption that the comparative enterprise is an organic phenomenon that exists objectively in the natural world, readily accessible to the religionist's gaze. It is the job of the professional religionist, in other words, to encounter religion[1] at face value and, from this encounter, make meaningful statements about some isolated and privileged zone of faith and experience. Finally, based on this, the religionist – at least according to this model – is able to derive conclusions about humanity. At the background of Cantwell Smith's discussion is the thought and writings of Mircea Eliade, especially his concept of the irreducibility of the sacred. In the following passage, from his preface to the English translation of *Patterns in Comparative Religion*, Eliade compares this irreducibility to understanding *Madame Bovary*:

> [A] religious phenomenon will only be recognized as such if it is grasped at its own level, that is to say, if it is studied as something religious. To try to grasp the essence of such a phenomenon by mean of physiology, psychology, sociology, economics, linguistics, art or any other study is false; it misses the one unique and irreducible element in it – the element of the sacred... Because religion is human it must for that very reason be something social, something linguistic, something economic – you cannot think of man apart from language and society. But it would be hopeless to try and explain religion in terms of any one of those basic functions which are really no more than another way of saying that man is. It would be as futile as thinking you could explain [the novel] *Madame Bovary* by a list of social, economic, and political facts; however true, they do not affect it as a work of literature (1958, i; cf. 1959, 209–10).

In his well-known *The Meaning and End of Religion* (1991 [1962]), Cantwell Smith argues that even though they lack insight into the experiential nature of religion that is available to the devotee, scholars of religion must take it for granted, on faith if you will, that "religious experiences" exist. He frames it thus:

> I certainly do not deny, then, that Christians in the religious life have something in common – or Muslims, or any group, or indeed all men together. What rather I am asserting (comfortably both to the historian, who cannot see the common element, and to the man of faith, who therein can) is that what they have in common lies not in the tradition that introduces them to transcendence, not by their faith by which they personally respond, but in that to which they respond, the transcendent itself (1991 [1962], 192).

3 Tensions Past, Tensions Future

The way that Cantwell Smith proposes to go about understanding this "response to the transcendent" is, as he tells us in a publication written at roughly the same time as *The Meaning and End of Religion*, to study the faith of others (1962, 14–16):

> My aspiration is not to get you to understand, for instance, Buddhism; but to help you to understand Buddhists. And this means, basically, trying to help you see the world as a Buddhist sees it. Another way of expressing the same point is to say that I do not propose to talk about other men's customs and beliefs, but about other men's faith (1962, 17).

For Cantwell Smith, religion is something that is not to be interrogated, but exists a priori. Religion is that which gives deep meaning to practitioners' lives from the top down, but is never actively constructed from the bottom up. This must be understood, but never explained. In terms of Islam, Cantwell Smith, like many discussed in this study, operates on the assumption that a monolithic Islam exists and that, as such, it can be readily studied by observant Muslims and those sympathetic to their faith commitments. This often involves appealing to something unique in the religious heritage of Islam, some thing or belief that successfully and essentially differentiates it from other religions. For instance:

> Islam is in every sense a great affair. The Muslim in Lahore, or in Samarqand or Kano, does not feel isolated, but is vividly conscious of belonging to a living community spread across the globe... Not only does the call [to prayer] put him effectively in a setting that stretches far in space, from Java to Morocco. Also, it places him in an historical setting, stretching back in time, to a past glory of which he is both aware and proud. The same call to prayer, with its serene dignity, has been repeated five times each day over the centuries. By it, and the faith that it expresses, the Muslim is firmly related to a past that stands imposingly behind him, bequeathing him traditions and institutions that have stood the test of age, and are bound to patterns of life that made his ancestors great (1981, 4).

With passages such as this, Cantwell Smith assumes a stability existing deep in the heart of every religion, a unified set of meanings that moves across time and space that practitioners simply subscribe to and whence they connect to pre-established concepts. The reality, as I have tried to suggest numerous times, is that this is most likely not the case at all. A Muslim in seventh-century Arabia would probably not recognize or share the same values as a Muslim living in twenty-first-century Montreal. The latter may well tell us that she shares an existential or experiential affinity with Muslims across time and space, but it is our job as disinterested scholars of Islam to see concepts such as "existential affinities" as related to the nostalgia of authenticity in the light of various social, cultural, and political impediments. Cantwell Smith, of course, had to take such claims at face value because his hermeneutic demanded that the only things that he could academically say about Muslims would have to be agreed upon by Muslims themselves. This in itself is a problematic statement given the fact that it assumes that all Muslims (e.g., Sunnis, Shi'is, Sufis, Isma'ilis, Ahmidiyyas) could or would agree on a set of universally valid criteria.

Although I have called into question both Cantwell Smith's comparative enterprise and his understanding of Islam, his approach has certainly left its mark on both fields. For example, when he set up the graduate program in Islamic studies at McGill, he defined the degree regulations for the PhD as follows:

> [The PhD's] ambition would be to encompass something of the substance of both Western and Islamic traditions, and also something of the form of both... In the matter of form, [the candidate] should not only satisfy the principle of a Western doctorate, but also produce work that would maintain continuity with the Islamic tradition. It is the task...of the Institute to strive for the construction of new forms that will subsume but transcend the present pattern on both sides: new forms, that is, that will neither betray the Western academic tradition nor distort the Islamic. The product of research must be relevant to both, significant to both, and cogent in both... [The] thesis should be recognizable in both traditions as a constructive advance (W.C. Smith 1959, 52, n. 41).

According to such criteria, anyone graduating with a doctorate in Islamic studies at McGill would have had to have spoken at least two conceptual languages, that of the Western academic tradition(s) (whatever this may consist of) and presumably, though it is never fully spelled out, that of traditional Islamic scholarship. This gets very tricky, not to mention extremely ambiguous. To whom exactly is the graduate supposed to speak? To whom does she market her dissertation when it comes out as a book by presumably a university press? Since there exists no real autonomous theoretical discourse devoted to the academic study of religion in the so-called Islamic tradition, the PhD graduate from McGill must essentially speak the discourse of Muslim theologians. This, more often than not, involves taking a set of manuscripts, establishing a critical edition, and then explicating the text internally and by connecting it to other Islamic texts.

Based on the approach that I am adopting in this study, this is a conceptual nightmare. It is simply impossible to dismantle traditional understandings of religion, its will to power and self-legitimation, if one has to produce work that must be judged according to those whom we study. This influence of Cantwell Smith has, I would argue, been problematic to the academic integrity of the critical study of Islam. This becomes even more problematic when it is remembered that the Institute of Islamic

Studies at McGill has been responsible for producing many, if not the majority, of Islamicists who held (and continue to hold) positions in religious studies departments throughout North America. This is one of the largest handicaps, I submit, facing the successful integration of the study of Islam and theory and method in the study of religion.

Perhaps to its credit, the Institute at McGill no longer requires its graduates to contribute to the Islamic tradition of learning or thinking about religion. However, a perusal of their new requirements (Institute of Islamic Studies 2006) still shows a resistance to an interdisciplinary or multidisciplinary approach to Islamic data. The operating assumption seems to be that other disciplines actually get in the way of a proper understanding of such data rather than aid in its illumination. In the following passage, for example, a potential student's desire to take courses in other departments, including that of religious studies, is regarded as a hindrance as opposed to any sort of aid to thinking about Islam:

> In cases in which the student's research plans and interests justify such arrangements the student at the Ph.D. level may take no more than one full-year course (i.e. 6 credits) in other departments or units of the university. [It is possible for a Ph.D. student to take a maximum of 2 full-year courses (i.e. equivalent to 12 credits) from outside the Institute: 6 credits maximum in the M.A. programme plus 6 credits maximum in the Ph.D. programme.] Students wishing to do a substantial amount of work outside the Institute of Islamic Studies and have it credited to their programme should seek permission by directing a petition to the Director of the Institute who will present the matter to the staff for a decision. *Permission to do work outside the Institute of Islamic Studies shall not be construed as grounds to ignore or neglect any area of Islamic Studies that is relevant to students' research or important to the full development of their knowledge in Islamic Studies* (Institute of Islamic Studies 2006, 2; my italics).

To reiterate, such an approach to Islamic data – *viz.*, that there exists such data naturally in the world irrespective of how such groups appeal to it in manifold constructions – poses many problems for Islam's smooth integration into the field of religious studies, which of course assumes that a discipline called by this name exists and is healthy (something that it most decidedly is not). No religious tradition can be viewed as so unique that it does not require the heuristic and conceptual tools supplied by cognate departments. If Islam is impervious to the critical models currently being employed in the study of religion and/or culture, this says less about the religious tradition than the imaginations of those scholars doing research on it. The result of both Cantwell Smith's approach to comparison and the way in which the academic study of Islam was set up at McGill has led to an unfortunate unwillingness on the part of scholars of Islam to employ the vocabularies and categories provided by the critical discourse of those in religious studies who regard "religion" as nothing more or less than a byproduct of human socio-rhetorical activity.

Lest Cantwell Smith's legacy be confined to that of the Institute of Islamic Studies at McGill, it is interesting to examine similar requirements for doctoral students at Harvard's Center for the Study of World Religions. There, a similar model is in place. Unlike at McGill, however, the "comparative model" seems to be constructed into the very heart of the program. For example in the "Option One: Comparative" track at the Center for the Study of World Religions, we read even today that

> While there is a comparative element in all advanced study of religion, the work under this Option makes it explicit in that the student chooses for comparison two religious traditions (see list above), one to be the major, one the minor. As historical complexes are by nature comparative, they should not be chosen for comparison in an Option I program. Therefore, one could do an Option I program comparing Christianity and Hinduism, but not Christianity and South Asia. Nor could one compare the Modern West and South Asia, for example. *In view of the comparative emphasis, a student should select as the major a tradition to which he or she is not personally related by commitment and/or cultural affiliation. The minor tradition chosen will normally be the one to which the candidate is related* (http://fas.harvard.edu/~csrel/doctoral/prospective/phd.html; my italics).

According to this passage, comparative work at Harvard seems to be based on the assumption that there exists such a thing as comparison in the study of religion, that it exists naturally in the world, that religion exists independently of culture, and that it is the scholar's job to uncover the implicit or explicit connections. Moreover, the basis for this comparison is a "minor" tradition to which the candidate is "related by commitment and/or cultural affiliation."

Marshall Hodgson's Conscientious Objections

Marshall G. S. Hodgson (1922–1968), called by some the "greatest American Islamicist," taught Islamic history and civilization at the University of Chicago before his untimely death at the age of forty-seven. His massive three-volume *The Venture of Islam: Conscience and History in a World Civilization* was published posthumously in 1974 from his original manuscript and notes. It is a work of uncommon nuance, self-reflexivity, and vision. Despite the fact that it is in continual print, its length, complexity, and denseness unfortunately make it difficult to implement in the undergraduate classroom.

3 Tensions Past, Tensions Future

In the lengthy introduction to the work, a must-read for any serious student or scholar of the field, Hodgson is extremely critical of two emphases that he feels have been detrimental to the study of Islam: Arabism and philology.

> This Arabistic and philological bias is reflected in book after book and article after article; not least in the *Encyclopedia of Islam*, where many entries discuss more the word (usually in its Arabic form even if it is derived, say, from Persian) than the substance; and present data from Egypt and Syria as if for Islamdom as a whole (1974, 40).

The philological bias, according to Hodgson, has also created a tendency to focus on "high culture" at the expense of "more local or lower-class social conditions; and within the high culture, to be preoccupied with religious, literary, and political themes, which are most accessible to a philological approach" (1974, 41). Hodgson, then, was responsible for trying to force a shift from a philological-based study of Islam to one that was based on understanding the universal themes and cultural patterns of Islamic history conceived in very broad terms.

Despite Hodgson's concerns to liberate the study of Islam from the tyranny of philology, he nevertheless falls back on the concept that religion is protected by the inner life of individuals, the so-called "conscience" of his subtitle. According to Bryan S. Turner:

> Islam as a religion and social system was treated as an adventure of the inner, personal conscience which created an external, impersonal civilization, the conscience was treated as a creative, irreducible activity in the history of private individuals for whom social, political and economic factors ("ecological circumstances") operated "merely [to] set the limits of what is possible" (Hodgson 1974, 26). The consequence of such an approach was to provide, so to speak, a religious niche or hiding-place within which "faith" could remain sociologically immune (1994, 54).

For Hodgson, "conscience" is rooted in the personal piety of the individual and it is ultimately this that nourishes and subsequently gives life-blood to both religions and civilizations (1974, 25–30, 359–64). For example, Hodgson argues that

> Personal piety is in some ways but a small part of religion. Yet it is the core of it. For it is in personal devotion (whether by way of the usual rituals, or otherwise) that the cosmic dimension is entered upon which makes religion religious; and hence that the whole structure of a religious community ultimately justifies itself. Accordingly, what we call personal piety or devotion plays a key role in civilization as a whole, at least wherever religious traditions are of major importance (1974, 360).

Although Hodgson is able to argue personal piety plays a large role in motivating human history, it is ultimately based on inner experience and thus cannot be quantified or explained using sociological or other methods. On the contrary, he defines religion as "a *life-orientational* experience or behavior in the degree to which it is focused on the role of a *person in an environment felt as a cosmos*; a focus which has normally entailed some experience of the numinous and/or some notion of cosmic transcendence, and efforts to respond thereto" (1974, 362–63; italics in original). In defining religion in these terms, Hodgson, in a footnote, favorably cites Eliade's *The Sacred and the Profane* (Hodgson 1974, 363 n. 1).

For Hodgson, it is the private nature of faith, piety, or conscience – in many ways evocative of what we saw in the work of Cantwell Smith above – that truly drives history. Although it is possible to explain Islam as a set of public and cultural phenomena, it is faith and all of its internal baggage that "are private, having an integrity uncontaminated by sociological factors" (Turner 1994, 56).[2]

This approach to religion enters the discipline of Islamic studies at a particular historical moment. This moment occurred when certain scholars of Islam began to pick up the trail of *sui generis* religion that was currently being dropped by phenomenologists such as Mircea Eliade. As long as we are cognizant of this fact, there is no real problem. My fear, however, is that we begin to lose sight of the genealogy, mistaking its ideological assertions for historical truth claims, thereby thinking that Islam, or any other religion for that matter, really possesses an antagonism between inner faith and the outer workings of history.

Fazlur Rahman and Islamic Reform

Since the academic study of Islam within departments of religious studies is roughly only thirty years old, it is a subdiscipline that is in many ways still attempting to discover itself, its narratives still very much in progress. If Cantwell Smith and Hodgson were two of the earliest examples of the attempt to integrate the study of Islam within the broadly defined disciplinary parameters of religious studies, one of the first Muslim scholars to attempt this was Fazlur Rahman (1911–1988). Rahman was born in Hazara, now in Pakistan, and received his doctorate at Oxford University, studying with, among others, Richard Walzer, and writing a thesis on the eleventh-century Islamic philosopher Avicenna, subsequently published as *Avicenna's Psychology: An English Translation of Kitāb al-Najāt, Book II,*

3 Tensions Past, Tensions Future

chapter VI (1981). Not content to examine Avicenna as a Muslim thinker, Rahman connected his thought to the Greek Aristotelian, Middle Platonic, and Neoplatonic philosophical traditions. Only by understanding Avicenna's debt to the Greeks, argued Rahman, could one fully appreciate his contribution to Islamic Thought.

After teaching at McGill's Institute of Islamic Studies until 1961, he returned to Pakistan to take up the directorship of the Central Institute of Islamic Research. The goal of this Institute was to begin the process of reforming and modernizing Pakistan's education curriculum. Like many Muslim scholars who would come after him, Rahman saw himself as someone who could reform the Islamic tradition from within. Unfortunately, his attempts at reform were not successful and he had to flee Pakistan in fear of his life. He subsequently ended up at the University of Chicago where he was appointed the Harold H. Swift Distinguished Service Professor of Islamic Thought. Although Rahman taught a generation of students about Islam in the Divinity School at Chicago (see the essays in Waugh and Denny 1998), his appointment was in Middle Eastern studies. This appointment, as Richard Martin argues, was indicative of the field in the 1970s:

> the academic home of Islamic religious studies at major graduate institutions in North America is Middle Eastern (and to a lesser extent South Asian) area studies. Thus, the study of Islamic religion often assumes the peripheral status of being "cross-listed." When it comes to Islam, students seeking courses and dissertation committee members must change venues. This peculiar academic doctrine that outsiders to Middle Eastern and Islamic studies are ill-prepared to understand Islam – its texts, languages, and religious phenomena – lends Islamic and Middle Eastern studies their aura of uniqueness. Only insiders – Muslims according to some, Middle East specialists according to others – are qualified to speak. It is a form of academic mysticism (Martin 1998, 253).

In the writings of Fazlur Rahman we witness the tensions between the Islamicist as scholar and as reformer, as religionist and area studies expert. For instance, in the preface to his *Islam* (1979 [1966]), still widely used in introductory courses to this day, Rahman sets out as his goal:

> The writer is of the view that it is simply impossible to "describe" a religion and particularly his own faith and fail to convey to the reader anything of that *inner intensity of life which constitutes that faith*. This book is, therefore, meant equally for Western and Muslim readers. The Muslim should learn to look more objectively at his religious history, particularly at how Islam has fared at his hands, and the non-Muslim should learn to know something of what Islam does to a Muslim from the inside (ix; my italics).

Rahman here takes a page from Cantwell Smith's institutionalization of the concept that a scholar of Islam must speak to both Muslims and non-

Muslims by making a contribution to western and Islamic thought. This approach, as I tried to suggest above, leads to all sorts of hermeneutical contortions: What happens when the two audiences do not overlap? Can one speak to one who is interested in socio-rhetorical formation at the same time as one does to the pious believer? Does the believing Muslim who wants to understand something of his or her own "faith tradition" have the same concerns as the religionist who contends that faith is nothing more or less than a quest for legitimation based on a number of political and ideological concerns?

Also invoked in this statement is the seemingly perennial claim to some set of amorphous and inner experiences of Muslims (in this case, the author himself). Based on appeals to such a set of experiences, the author is able to speak from a position of authority, one that it is implied that the non-Muslim reader must accept on little more than (a different kind of) faith. But if Rahman speaks as someone who believes in the existence of something called faith, he also speaks in his academic writings as a Muslim reformer. Islam, according to him, is in dire need of reform as it rubs up against modernity. For him, as a scholar of medieval philosophy, this must involve a return to critical thinking:

> One should perhaps say, therefore, that Islamic theology/philosophy has to be rebuilt afresh on the basis of the Qur'ān, rather than reconstructed from this medieval heritage. How does one reconstruct, for example, the medieval theological doctrines of God and His attributes?…but the greatest desideratum of medieval Islamic thought is in the field of ethics. One cannot point to a single work of ethics squarely based upon the Qur'ān…although [some ethical works] have been, to a greater or lesser extent, integrated with the Qur'ān, they cannot be regarded essentially as expressions of it. *Even the Hadith literature, although correct in its essential spirit, must because of its diffuse and abstract character be collated with and streamlined by the Qur'ān. Such a work of ethics will represent the essence of the Qur'ān, for the Qur'ān is primarily an ethical teaching (with a theological base), and not a book of law* (1979 [1966], 257; my italics).

Here Rahman implies that the study of the medieval Islamic heritage is not simply a scholarly enterprise. On the contrary, it represents the building blocks for developing a new understanding of Islam, one that is rational and one that although firmly embedded in modernity, nonetheless still has one foot in the Qur'ān:

> The development of a theology/philosophy, ethics, law and social science based on the Qur'ān and the model of the Prophet must, in fact, in some sense precede any actual undertaking of educational reform… If the Muslim can successfully attempt this task, he will have implemented the basic élan of the Qur'ān and saved mankind from what seems to be nothing less than suicide… (1979, 264–65; see further 1982[3]).

Rahman, despite being an excellent scholar in the intellectual history of Islam, shows us that his real interest here is not reading medieval philosophical sources solely for their intrinsic interest. Rather, his goal seems to be much more grandiose and at the same time impossible: reinvigorating the spirit of Islam, whatever that may be, in order to bring about a renaissance that can, to use his own words, "save mankind from what seems to be nothing less than suicide." I say impossible because Rahman here assumes that there is some authentic kernel that runs throughout Islamic history and that, once discovered, it can be used as a panacea to cure an ailing Islam of its current sickness. On a phenomenological level this discourse differs little from that of Islamists.

Indeed, so similar is Rahman's monolithic construction of Islam and Muslim identity that he can isolate the reason for Islam's degeneration in one particular group, the anti-intellectual Sufis:

> What has Sufism given on the positive side? There is no doubt that it has created certain great personalities from time to time – men of outstanding moral, spiritual and, in some cases, even intellectual caliber. But these are isolated cases… To the masses, the Sufi spiritual ideal offered an escape from the uninviting realities of life – economic hardship, social imbalance, political uncertainties. But this it did at the expense of the Islamic ideal of a social order. Instead of this moral-social order it taught people certain techniques of auto-suggestion and hypnotism and an excessive indulgence in an altogether emotionalized religion which can only be described as mass hysteria. It is this phenomenon – the total effect of superstitionism, miracle-mongering, tomb-worship, mass-hysteria and, of course, charlatanism – that we have described above as the moral and spiritual debris from which Muslim society has to be reclaimed for Islam (1981 [1952], 246).

This statement, presented in an introductory textbook on Islam meant for North American students, differs little from the ideology that drives Islamic fundamentalists, including groups such as the Taliban, which put the blame on Sufism (not to mention Israel and the US) for Islam's current plight. Moreover, exactly like Rahman, such groups negotiate around the "mass-hysteria" of Sufism by manufacturing a normative Islam that they cull from earlier sources, an authentic expression of faith to which one can somehow return and that magically presents a panacea.

The study of Islam has been continually mired in extra-scholarly matters. Previously we have witnessed how this took the form of Jewish reform, Arab identity movements, the desire to carve out space in interdisciplinary programs by claiming expertise in the "Islamic mind," and appeals to an inner understanding based on explicating an amorphous set of faith concerns. With Rahman's scholarly agenda, we see yet another aspect of this: that of a Muslim reformer with a PhD in Islamic studies from a western university seeking to effect change in the Islamic world based on his or her academic understanding of a monolithic Islam. Rather than conceptualize Islam as a broad canopy that covers diverse and often contradictory sets of commitments, expressions, and ideologies, the approach offered by Rahman seeks to single out one such set and make it normative.

The quest for normativity, the desire to create a true form of any religion, and then be a proponent of it, is not a scholarly endeavor. There is certainly nothing wrong with such an approach; for all I know it is even a desideratum, at least if one is a theologian. What I draw attention to here, though, is the contradictory aims, methods, and audiences such works generate when theology masquerades as a, much less the, critical discourse devoted to religion. It may be one thing to label Sufism as "charlatanic" in a theological book devoted to clarifying Islamic principles and directed towards a Muslim reading audience; it is something altogether different, however, to make the same case in an introductory textbook used in North American university classes devoted to the study of Islam in a religious studies environment. This confusion of intention results in a confusion in method. The results, needless to say, are harmful to the safe integration of Islam within religious studies.

As the study of Islam began to gravitate out of Middle Eastern or Near Eastern studies programs it has become increasingly associated with politics of identity and representation. While, once again, there is nothing inherently wrong with such an agenda, it is nevertheless necessary to clarify it, to be aware of what it can do and what it cannot do. In order to show that the scholar of Islam *qua* reformer is not just a thing of the past, let me quote briefly from two works that I think exemplify such a position today. The first comes from Omid Safi's edited volume entitled *Progressive Muslims*. In his introduction to the work, a collection of essays by leading scholars of Islam, he writes:

> It is our hope that the book you hold in your hand marks a new chapter in the rethinking of Islam in the twenty-first century. Our aim has been to envision a socially and politically active Muslim identity that remains committed to ideals of social justice, pluralism, and gender justice... Our aim is to open up a place in the wider spectrum of Islamic thought and practice for the many Muslims who aspire to justice and pluralism. This will entail both producing concrete intellectual products and changing existing social realities (2003, 6).

The second comes from Ebrahim Moosa, *Ghazālī and the Poetics of Imagination*. In this work, Moosa, like Rahman,[4] uses a key figure in Islamic intellectual history, Abū Hāmid al-Ghazālī (d. 1111), as a catalyst to rethink Islam's relationship to modernity.

3 Tensions Past, Tensions Future

> If there is any concrete lesson to be learned from Ghazālī's experience, then it is this: the end to the enduring search for solutions to humanity's existential crises can be found in the creativity of the human spirit. Ghazālī is a sterling example of someone who conquered the odds and found a path out of depressing personal despair and social anomie. In the triumph of the spirit, Ghazālī stands out as a beacon of hope in times of anguish: he led with imagination in order to overcome ignorance; he preferred originality to imitation, and favored renewal over complacency… Surely, perfection is not what we seek from an exemplary figure, least of all from Ghazālī. However, what we do seek in our heroes and models is a depth of humanity, vision, and compassion in which we can find echoes of our own hopes and aspirations, our own various communities and societies (Moosa 2005, 28).

Let me reiterate that there is certainly nothing inherently wrong with either a monograph devoted to pluralism, gender, social justice, or to showing how a medieval thinker can cure the ills of modern Islam. Indeed, such works, given the current historical moment, are probably necessary. However, the problem occurs when such apologetic works either portray themselves or are portrayed by others as objective works of scholarship. It is such cross purposes that lead to an unwillingness on the part of those *within* the discipline to interrogate a tradition using the apparatus supplied by critical discourses outside of their field. The results have been very problematic.

4 We Study Muslim Constructions, Not Muslims, Right?

It is true that we instinctively recoil from seeing an object to which our emotions and our affections are committed handled by the intellect as any other object is handled. The first thing the intellect does with an object is to class it along with something else. But any object that is infinitely important to us and awakens our devotion feels to us also as if it must be *sui generis* and unique. Probably a crab would be filled with a sense of personal outrage if it could hear us class it without ado or apology as a crustacean, and thus dispose of it. "I am no such thing" it would say; "I am MYSELF, MYSELF alone" (James 1990 [1902], 17).

When one permits those whom one studies to define the terms in which they will be understood, suspends one's interest in the temporal and contingent, or fails to distinguish between "truths," "truth-claims," and "regimes of truth," one has ceased to function as a historian or scholar. In that moment, a variety of roles are available: some perfectly respectable (amanuensis, collector, friend and advocate), and some less appealing (cheerleader, voyeur, retailer of import goods). None, however, should be confused with scholarship (Lincoln 1996, 227).

In the previous chapter I charted the migration of a particular discourse in vogue among students of religion into the academic study of Islam. The result was that many Islamicists began to feel more institutionally at home in departments devoted to the study of religion than in the traditional centers of Middle Eastern studies. This new level of comfort within religious studies seems to have been based on the latter discourse's privileging of interiority, faith and essence over more tangible and quantifiable entities such as social forms and cultural work. All of the privileged terms in the last sentence, of course, were concepts that could not be verified by independent means, but were nevertheless assumed to exist by those who claimed expertise for themselves in this area.

From an analytical point of view, this relationship between the academic study of Islam *qua* religion and the discipline of religious studies has not been a particularly productive one. The latter discourse, especially its emphases on amorphous qualities such as experience and faith, carried in its wake a whole host of nebulous and unchecked assumptions that tended (and still continue) to masquerade as axioms. One of this discourse's most egregious oversights is the way it posits the stability of concepts such as identity or religion through any number of temporal and geographical contexts. The idea that such concepts may, for example, be patchworks of crosscutting and often contradictory associations is rarely entertained.[1] Although it is acknowledged that historical forms may ebb and flow, many who buy into this *sui generis* discourse nevertheless maintain that the faith of religious practitioners somehow remains constant. This theory, as many of the examples to be discussed in this chapter demonstrate, would come to play a large role in defining the study of Islam. Despite recent attempts to undermine the model, to expose its genealogical and crypto-theological baggage, most scholars of Islam have largely been impervious to this critique.

Why were and are scholars of Islam so quick to buy into this essentialist discourse? This is a complicated question and one possible answer likely resides in the field's genealogy, especially the debates surrounding Orientalism and who qualifies to represent Muslims, the perennial Other. The study of philology, its privileging of the textual over the social, led many to gravitate naturally to a simplistic adoption of inner experience over the perceived outer form or husk of ritual, culture, or history. Regardless of the actual origins of this discourse in Islamic studies, its legacy has been debilitating, with the end result that our take on Islamic data is often obscured. By focusing on understanding over explanation, scholars of Islam have largely avoided asking hard questions of their data. Although not referring specifically to Islamic studies, the comments of J. Samuel Preus are nonetheless appropriate:

> It seems that the lack of interest in explaining religion stems from a combination of personal commitments, apologetic interests, and political convenience as much as from the "scientific" modesty often expressed by religious writers. "Religious studies" as it is normally carried on seems comfortable with a quasi-theological or metaphysical "solution" (or paradigm), by which the origins or causes of religion are placed beyond investigation on the ground that the source of religion is "transcendent." From such a perspective it is both unnecessary and impossible to advance any further toward explaining religion (Preus 1987, xviii).

In addition to this confusion of understanding with explanation, there exists an implicit hierarchy at work in the way scholars of Islam refract various times and geographical areas (see Hughes 2004b, 342–43). Despite the implicit criticism of philology, I nevertheless contend that textual study and all of the assumptions that go with it still drive the study of Islam in religious studies departments. This no doubt stems from the fact that places like the Islamic Studies Institute at McGill have played such a large role in training Islamicists who subsequently became and still become faculty members in departments of religious studies. Implicit in such programs, as I have shown elsewhere, is the assumption that there is some vaguely defined noumenal Islam that exists in its purest or most stable form in the Arabian peninsula, followed respectively by Persia, North Africa, South Asia, and finally North America and Europe (Hughes 2004b, 342–43). The further one moves away from the epicenter, the less likely one is to encounter the "authentic." Moreover, the "real" Islam is most readily accessed in classical texts (e.g., eighth to twelfth centuries). Here philologists and Islamists share the same basic operating assumption that there exists an "Islam" that resides in texts and that this "Islam" is somehow uncorrupted by the various cultures, local customs, and superstitions with which it comes into contact (Hughes 2004b, 343). These assumptions can be seen today in both the way graduate programs are set up and in the accounts provided by textbooks meant to introduce undergraduates (and the general reading public) to Islam.

In order to test this hypothesis, the present chapter will provide an analysis of several such textbooks written by professional Islamicists that purport to be introductions to Islamic data. Because so many of these textbooks reproduce the same concerns, doing their utmost to make sure that the reader is well acquainted with the faith and experiences of Muslims, they do little more than provide color commentary to what Muslims believe and say that they are doing. This should not, and here I refer to the quotation from Bruce Lincoln that begins this chapter "be confused with scholarship." Here it is worth pointing out that we can, for example, introduce students to the historical Jesus and the ideological implications of oral Torah at the introductory level, but rarely are Islamicists willing to entertain the historical Muhammad or the ideological implications of the various legal schools and the use of hadith at this level (or any other, for that matter).

Charles Adams and the Imperviousness of Islamic Data

Perhaps as good a way as any to enter into the problematic that this chapter seeks to address is with a quotation by Charles Adams, a graduate of the history of religions program at the University of Chicago in the early 1960s, and subsequent professor of Islamic studies at the Institute in McGill University. In an autobiographical statement, Adams writes of his initial excitement at the prospects of combining the critical discourse of religious studies with Islamic data:

> I advanced into the Islamics field with the expectations that a deeper knowledge of what scholars had done and were doing in the History of Religions would prove to be among the most valuable of resources for the work that lay ahead. I

understand my growing interest in the religious life of the Muslim community as a specification of a more general interest in the religious life of mankind as a whole (1967, 177).

Before unpacking Adams's assumptions here it is worth mentioning briefly the forum in which Adams's autobiographical musings occur. To commemorate the one-hundred-year anniversary of the founding of the Divinity School at the University of Chicago a series of conferences were held to "demonstrate the present vitality of the study of religion today" (Brauer 1967, vi). These conferences, according to McCutcheon, were instrumental in the formation and articulation of something that would hereafter become the sole domain of the expert in religious studies. This irreducible phenomenon – frequently referred to as "religion" or "the sacred" – was to define the religionist, whose sole job it now became to understand (but never explain, to recall Preus's phraseology) something defined as "religious experience." This would differentiate the religionist from what other scholars were doing (or not doing) in cognate disciplines (McCutcheon 2003, 67–70). As volume one in a projected eight-volume series entitled "Essays in Divinity," Brauer states that the goal of the collection in which Adams's essay appears is the development "of a methodology adequate to interpret and understand the data of religion" (1967, ix). Here Brauer, and this is something that is indicative of the essays that comprise the volume as a whole, signals his desire to find an appropriate method to take religion seriously. The idea of taking religion seriously, i.e., not reducing it to other phenomena, is of course a "codeword for the non reductive argumentation on *sui generis* religion" (McCutcheon 2003, 65).[2]

Returning to Adams's comments, despite his initial sense of optimism, he subsequently discovered that the history of religions had largely failed to meet his expectations. In fact, he argues that the potentially promising relationship between Islamic studies and the history of religions, or religious studies, failed to materialize. Rather than look to either the field of Islamic studies or perhaps his own theoretical and/or methodological shortcomings, Adams puts all of the blame on the academic study of religion. To paraphrase his arguments, these two disciplinary frameworks speak different conceptual vocabularies and are thus seemingly "impervious" to one another. He then concludes:

> For the student of Islam…the succession of emphases and the direction of development in the History of Religions has had little direct meaning…the historical stuff of Islamic religiousness is extraordinarily, one may say almost perversely, impervious to significant analysis along the lines which the majority of historians of religions have followed and are following (1967, 181–82).

Adams's comments here get to the heart of my study. Let me put to one side the assumptions of the "history of religions," especially its indebtedness to the problematic work of those like Wach and Eliade. Instead, I want to focus on how Adams intimates that attempts to import a larger analytical model to understand or problematize Islamic data is incorrect, precisely because the latter is somehow regarded as beyond a particular mode of analysis. In other words, he works on the assumption that there is something inherently unique about his data, and that this uniqueness somehow prevents it from being comprehended using the conceptual frameworks of other disciplines in either the humanities or social sciences. This hermeneutic, as I argued in the previous chapter, entered the discourse of Islamic studies in the 1960s and 70s as scholars of Islam began either to be employed in or come under the spell of the various categories employed in departments of religious studies. Worried at the prospects of reducing Islamic data to one manifestation or one particular subset of a more general pattern, to use Eliade's language, scholars such as Adams felt compelled to argue for Islam's, and not just religion's, uniqueness.

Again bracketing what Adams means by history of religions or even what its mandate was (in the 1960s) or should be today, he makes a number of problematic assumptions and/or implications. First, and perhaps most strange, Adams's criticisms are largely idiosyncratic. Based on his *own personal experiences* of working in both Islamic studies and religious studies, he does not *feel* that they go well together. In itself this is problematic owing to the unverifiability of the idiosyncratic. Why should we believe him based on his own impressions of this field? Adams only mentions one scholar of Islam that he is critical of: Ignaz Goldziher (1850–1921) who, given his dates, hardly counts as part of religious studies' failure to capture the imaginations of Islamicists. Other than the one reference to Goldziher, Adams does not connect his work to anyone else (on the importance of doing this, especially through footnotes, see Lincoln 1999, 208–209). Rather, we are left with a series of autobiographical reflections on what he thinks Islamicists should do.

Secondly, Adams, like so many who still work in the discipline of Islamic studies, confuses Islam *qua* a religion that provides emotive fulfillment for millions around the globe with an academic study that should ideally define Islam as nothing more than a series of sites of contention, thereby creating manifold mechanisms for the production of social and cultural identity. The two do not, and indeed cannot, be confused. For instance, he argues, undoubtedly following Cantwell Smith whose specter he would have encountered at McGill, that

One of the implications is that the Islamicist now finds himself drawn into personal relations with the modern representatives of the tradition he is endeavoring to study. But the responses that his work inevitably evokes, *if he is at all sensitive*, [sic] he is made vividly aware that he is speaking of historical events, developments, documents, personalities, and so on, that have a profound and immediate religious meaning in the lives of some millions of his contemporaries. Such a realization is sobering, *for it lays a moral responsibility upon anyone who ventures into the discussion of matters so charged with emotion and value. If he is alive to human feelings, he does not deal lightly and indifferently with things that represent the most precious insights and values of others* (Adams 1967, 188–89; my italics).

Here, Adams collapses scholarship into the murky domains of human sensitivity. Obviously scholars have a moral responsibility to something that in theory resembles or approximates standards of objectivity, but to argue that one's primary responsibility is to the objects of one's study and, more specifically, their "most precious insights" is extremely problematic. What this does, and this is certainly in keeping with the *sui generis* discourse emerging out of the University of Chicago in the 1960s and 1970s, is put such "insights" into a hermetically sealed enclosure. The result is that the scholar of Islam is only allowed to describe and provide color commentary to such insights, never question them or reduce them to other socio-rhetorical features.

Thirdly, Adams's comments are untenable even on the level of content. His claim that Islam is somehow impervious to the categories supplied by the academic study of religion is erroneous. For instance, he claims that analytical tropes such as sacral kingship and mythology, important in 1960s scholarship associated with the history of religions, do not really exist in Islam and, even if they did, would "not seem to offer access to the heart of *Islamic experience*" (1967, 182; his italics). It is, however, Adams's underscoring of "experience," not Islam's inherent imperviousness to myth, that prevents him from connecting his data to larger frameworks. In other words, Adams's situation of Islam, his definition of its quiddity, determines what he will find to be of importance.

Here I should mention two relatively recent works that seem to undermine Adams's claim here. Jaroslav Stetkevych, for instance, argues that scholars of Islam, like Muslims themselves, have always operated on the assumption that other than works such as the *Arabian Nights* there exists nothing of the legendary or the mythical in the sources of Islam (Stetkevych 1996, 1–3). Unwilling to buy into this narrative, Stetkevych himself admits that although the retrieval of such mythic and legendary elements in the Qurʾān may be difficult, this should certainly not occlude the possibility of such activity:

The problem with a number of these nuclei of myth was that in their survival in the new code, that is, through their co-optation by the Qur'ān (and the subsequent dogmatizing tradition), they were put to service of a rhetoric that was almost inimical to the "narrative" itself – this despite the qur'ānic claim that there they are being told in the best of narrative ways. That is, in the Qur'ān, narrative, and indeed everything else, is subordinated to the overarching rhetoric of salvation and damnation (Stetkevych 1996, 10).

Stetkevych implies that it is ideology, not the sources themselves, that prevents the type of analysis that Adams claims is impossible. In other words, the Qur'ān – not to mention the hadith, the Biography of the Prophet, and other works – are full of material that can be examined and analyzed using the critical methods supplied by other disciplinary frameworks. To say that it cannot is a theological and/or apologetical claim, an attempt, as Adams himself implies, to protect or defend the sensibilities of millions of Muslims, for whom the Qur'ān must be the unadulterated word of God and, as such, cannot possibly possess such mythopoeic fragments.

In a similar vein, some of my own work has argued that any attempt to remove Islam from its Near Eastern textual, linguistic, and cultural contexts is an act of violence that serves to obfuscate Islamic data, further contributing to its otherness. In particular I have argued that the goal of future research should not be to show the literary and religious discrepancies between the Near East and early Islam, but an analysis of "how the former permeates and influences the latter" (Hughes 2003, 262). So, for example, when Adams argues that categories such as myth, ritual, and divine kingship do not appear in Islam he is making an apologetical claim, one that many Muslims would no doubt endorse, but one that I contend is ultimately belied by the evidence. *Contra* Adams, I would argue that

> Islamic material in and of itself is not inherently impervious to the types of analyses and questions that the history of religions poses. Rather than take at face value such claims that Islam is conservative, austere or anti-mythological, we need to subject traditional data – e.g., the Qur'ān and the traditions surrounding it – to a new set of questions. The results will be of importance not only for shedding light on Islam, but also on the symbolic, metaphorical and cultural orbits of Muslims (Hughes 2003, 276).

Any attempt to make the case that Islam, or any other religion, should not or can not be understood using a larger set of analytical categories says much more about the person making such a claim than the claim itself. Here I refer to William James's crab that opens this chapter. Like the crab, we always want to claim that our data is singular, perhaps reflective of our own personalities, intellectual and emotional trajectories, etc. Yet, if the discourses associated with critical theory in religious studies tell us anything it is that such a perspective actually hinders our ability to understand how and why people legitimate themselves by appeals to various discourses, practices, institutions, and communities that they themselves have sublimated (see Lincoln 2003, 5–8).

Without getting into the problematic assumptions of what Adams thinks the emphases of religious studies are or should be, let alone that there exists something we can somehow neatly single out as religious data in the first place, we are still left with his central thesis that religious studies has somehow failed the study of Islam.[3] Can the theoretical apparatus of one over-arching discipline fail a set of data that are subsumed under it? Is Islam so essentially distinct from other religions (a claim frequently cited in Islamic theological literature) that it has to be examined using its own set of questions, employing its own modes of analysis? It is questions such as these that I now hope to problematize further by examining how and where non-specialists interested in Islam and Islamic data first encounter this tradition, in the introductory textbooks written by professional Islamicists.

Introducing Islam: The Beginner's Textbook

It is probably in the introductory textbook, more than anywhere else, that one is able to witness most clearly and perceptibly the various assumptions that a discipline holds dear. I here work on the notion that popular dissemination provides the public face of a field, thereby providing a window onto deeper theoretical presuppositions and genealogical baggage. If introductory textbooks are generally vague and often superficial, the introductory textbooks employed in religious studies are even worse, loaded with terms, categories, and assumptions that take us directly back to the founding of the discipline in North America in the late nineteenth and early twentieth centuries. Amorphous terms such as "sacred," "transcendent," and "quests" for "ultimate values" are often omnipresent in such books. The unfortunate result, of course, is that at the point at which we are potentially most able to do some good in getting students to think about religion (i.e., in large introductory classes where the overwhelming majority are non-majors) we are often at our most flaky, forced to rely on books that do little more than repeat to students what it is that religious people think they do when they assent to something that they refer to as religious (see the comments in McCutcheon 1997, ch. 3).

This is particularly problematic when it comes to introducing Islam. Islam, in many ways, provides an interesting challenge to introductory courses. For one thing, in the current global moment, it is a religion that is invoked, usually negatively, everywhere. Islam and Muslims, for example, are deemed responsible for the insecurity that many Americans and Britons feel. In such countries, one now often meets students whose friends and loved ones are fighting in Iraq or Afghanistan, and who are often in danger in such countries. Add to this the notion that, especially in the United States, Islam is somehow regarded as not really a "religion," but a violent movement established by a power-hungry nomad,[4] and it is clear that to understand this tradition one must dismantle certain prejudices.

Equally problematic is the fact that often in the general introduction courses to "Religions of the West" the instructor is often much more unfamiliar or uncomfortable with Islam and Islamic data. This makes the desire to fall back on essentialist categories (e.g., "Muslims do…"; "Muslims believe…") pervasive in such courses, often in ways that the instructor might not contemplate in the case of either Judaism or Christianity, although I certainly do not want to imply that such introductory textbooks do a first-rate job of analyzing Jewish and Christian data and then fail when it comes to Islam. On the contrary, the way introductory religious studies textbooks introduce all religions, not to mention the very study of religion, is one of the greatest failures currently facing our discipline.

When these two features are combined, the unfortunate result is that it becomes extremely difficult to introduce Islam using a non-Cantwell Smithian discourse. Yet, if all we do is provide color commentary to Muslim lives and self-understandings, Islamic studies has largely failed not only itself, but the broader set of critical discourses that attempt to deconstruct the religious, the spiritual, and the faith-based in favor of less amorphous and more socio-rhetorical categories. Although I shall suggest some possible solutions to get beyond this impasse in the final chapter of this study, let it suffice here to point out what I consider to be an extreme failure of nerve (on this trope, see more generally Wiebe 1984, 2006) among scholars when it comes to introducing Islam to non-specialists.

In the remainder of this chapter, I shall survey a number of textbooks responsible for introducing Islam in general courses within departments of religious studies. Such books have shaped and continue to shape the way students (some of whom will be the graduate students and professors of tomorrow) encounter and subsequently think about Islam. My thesis, as in keeping with the general tenor of this study, is that we have created a noumenal, essentialized Islam that is sanctioned by all sorts of implicit genealogical baggage. This baggage has made many lose sight of what it is that we should be doing. In other words, to talk about Islam, for example as one scholar does, as "a person's total submission to the will of

God, which gives the faithful inner peace and soundness of nature in this life and the expectation of safety from divine retribution in the life to come" (Ayoub 2002, 341) is not particularly helpful. Although such phraseology may well have utility for ecumenism or an inter-faith group, it does little when it comes to understanding how and why various actors and groups have historically identified with or appealed to something constructed as "Islam" to legitimate a particular ideology.

My goal in examining these introductory books is not to be pedantic or highly critical. On the contrary, it is to demonstrate that the discourse that I have examined in the previous chapters is not simply a historical relic; on the contrary, this discourse – its assumptions of faith, its reliance on an essentialism that moves through time and space, and to which Muslims simply and effortlessly either assent to or depart from – continues to form the ontological backdrop against which scholars of Islam construct, situate and think about their data.

Islam as Part of the "Holy Trinity": Introducing Western Religions

One of the most problematic features inherent to the myriad of textbooks that publishers throw at us each summer is their tacit ecumenical and liberal Protestant assumptions. These assumptions rather than help students give up their traditional beliefs about religion instead often reinforce them. Instead of challenging them, such books often conform to what students already think they know about religious phenomena. For instance, one of the most important building blocks in the historical formation of Islam was the Qur'ān. This book was instrumental in the legitimization of an emerging polity in seventh-century Arabia, one that was struggling to define itself over and against competing monotheisms in the region (e.g., various forms of Christianities and Judaisms). The quiddity of this contestation – for example that the earliest Muslims fasted during Yom Kippur and prayed facing Jerusalem – is often glossed over in favor of rather insipid phrases such as "Islam began to distinguish itself from Judaism" (Ayoub 2002, 346) or that the Jews "denied Muhammad's prophethood and message and cooperated with his Meccan enemies" (Esposito 2005 [1988], 15). Such phrasings do little to contribute to our understanding of the processes involved in proto-Islamic socio-rhetorical formation. Indeed such questions, let alone their answers, have largely fallen out of favor since Said's critique of Orientalism, where they are now understood as little more than the attempt by Western imperial powers, and their scholars, to undermine the Orient in general and Islam in particular (see Chapter 1).

Moreover, religious studies, when understood properly and not just as a form of color commentary, cannot work on the assumption that books fall from heaven. When we simply repackage and repeat the stories that Muslims (or Christians or Jews, etc.) tell themselves, we, as the quotation from Lincoln that begins this chapter so well arrticulates, move outside the domain of scholarship and into the murky realm of apologetics. There is nothing inherently wrong with the latter so long as it is clear that this is what the discourse is doing and does not masquerade as something objective, which it all too often does. In introducing the Qur'ān this is particularly problematic. For instance, we are often willing at the introductory level to talk about the redaction of the Hebrew Bible and the ideology of the emerging rabbinical classes in this process; likewise with the New Testament, we are often comfortable talking about the lost gospel of Q and the various redactional processes involved in group legitimation (e.g., Pauline, Johannine, Markan). Yet, when it comes to the Qur'ān, we tend to repeat platitudes that ignore such processes. How was the Qur'ān formed? What ideological processes went into this formation? How did much older oral traditions make their way into the document (as they did, for example, in the Hebrew Bible and the New Testament)?[5]

Let me leave aside the problematic nature of introducing students to the formation of the Qur'ān, but at the same time flag this issue as an important lacuna indicative of a larger problem within the field. And also let me reiterate that I am using such textbooks here as a mirror for how the discipline perceives itself, and thereby defines what it holds dear. In his chapter devoted to "The Islamic Tradition" – and in such books it is important to note that "tradition" or "religion" is always employed in the singular, never of course wanting to imply that an assumed essentialized message actually undergoes various permutations and contestations at various historical moments – Mahmoud Ayoub falls back on a conceptualization that we witnessed time and again in the previous chapter:

> The Qur'ān further makes an important distinction between Islam and faith. Outwardly, Islam is a religious, social, and legal institution, whose members constitute the worldwide Muslim *ummah* or community. *Īmān*, faith, is an inner conviction whose sincerity or insincerity God alone can judge, a commitment to a way of life in the worship of God and in moral relations with other persons (2002, 359).

Here, Ayoub, much like Hodgson before him, distinguishes between the outward forms of Islam and the inner soul that drives these forms through time, space, history, and geography. This body–soul dualism implies that things could not or should not be otherwise. In other words, the various outer forms of Islam are the way they are because of an inner spirit, providence, *Geist* or whatever that drives them. The theological overtones in such assumptions are unmistakable: Islam (again, never islams) is a given; it is a way of life that falls from heaven and that even if it manifests itself in different historical periods, inside it is always the same.

Yet, contrary to Ayoub, I would argue that all that we have to analyze are precisely these outward forms. There is quite simply no way to access the inner dimension of religion even if we assume that (1) it exists, and (2) we wanted to access it in the first place. Moreover, bracketing for the moment that we could access and then analyze such inner experiences, whose experiences would we choose? Whose become authoritative? Is it the Taliban general who closes a school for girls in Kandahar? Is it a lesbian Isma'ili in Toronto? The way to get out of this problem is to do what Ayoub does; namely, to speak in such vague terms about "Islamic faith" that it applies, at one the same time, to everyone and no one:

> Outwardly, the *shahādah* [the phrase by which a Muslim bears witness to God] legally safeguards a person's rights as a member of the Muslim community. Inwardly, however, it is meaningless unless it becomes a true expression of personal faith (*īmān*) and righteous living (*iḥsān*). Without this inner dimension of the *shahādah*, Islam loses its meaning as a faith tradition (2002, 361).

Such a statement takes us beyond the pale of the academic study of religion and firmly into the world of theology or, perhaps better, crypto-theology because it masquerades as belonging to the discourse of religious studies. Perhaps the blurb endorsing the book on the back cover written by Nathan M. Pusey, President Emeritus of Harvard, says it all: "This book should be required reading for every student *in theology*" (my italics).

Ayoub concludes his chapter in the volume by appealing to a particular form of Islam, what he calls "Islamic humanism" (2002, 454), as the future of *the* tradition. He writes that:

> Muslims can accomplish much in the West if they promote Islamic humanism and a spirit of trust allowing collaboration with their non-Muslim neighbors for greater justice and moral consciousness. There is still a significant need to change old images and ideas if future generations of Muslims in the West are to remain active as Muslims in a society that integrates Muslims and others (2002, 454).

The implication here is that Islam at its most adaptable and hence most authentic is an Islam that coincides most closely with liberal Western values. The emphasis on justice and moral consciousness, in other words, creates a palatable Islam for Western audiences (to whom the chapter is addressed). Implicit in Ayoub's comments is that the faith that he talked about earlier in the chapter is what endorses this universalist Islamic message; other, more particularistic constructions of Islam emerge from this discussion as somehow less than authentic. Once again, then, we see a scholar situate Islam against a number of extra-scholarly or intellectual concerns. The aim is not to examine how Muslim agents have historically appealed to sources to construct an Islam that they deem the most authentic, nor is it even to query the discourse of authenticity and the genealogies that follow in its wake. In fact, the scholar of Islam, as I have intimated throughout this study, often does precisely what Muslims have done historically: picked and chosen particular sources to create an Islam that is sublimated as an essence, to which subsequent constructions are held up and then deemed authentic or inauthentic as the case may be.

Having examined some of the ways that Islam is treated in textbooks that are meant to introduce students to the religions of the West, let me now turn my attention towards texts devoted solely to Islam. Although these works, usually meant to be used in courses such as "Introduction to Islam" or "Islamic Civilization," provide more depth than single sections, such as those by Ayoub, it will soon become readily apparent that these books differ little when it comes to essentialist assumptions about the nature of religion in general and Islam in particular.

Esposito's *Islam: The Straight Path*

In the revised third edition of his popular introductory textbook (2005 [1988]), John Esposito seeks to provide not only an introduction to Islamic faith and praxis, but also, especially post-9/11, a corrective to the stereotype that Islam endorses violence. Like many in the aftermath of 9/11, Esposito is interested in the rhetorics of faith and authenticity and how such categories can manufacture an image of Islam that conforms to liberal and Western ideals. Such a project may actually be a desideratum, but we have to be aware that it is no less a construction of Islam than that provided by those who say this tradition is inherently predisposed to violence.

Many Muslims, especially those not part of what Lincoln calls "maximalist micro-entities" (2003, 3–5), are more than comfortable with making an Islam conform to liberal Western ideals. The flaw, however, is to make this type of Islam normative, the standard by which to judge all competitors. This desire to create such an Islam, one from which various islams fall away, plays a large role in the rhetorics of faith that are, in turn, responsible for situating Islam in the modern world, in both scholarly and non-scholarly projects. This normative or authentic Islam, to quote from Esposito's *The Islamic Threat: Myth or Reality?* (1999 [1992]), also currently in its third edition, is always in danger of being subverted by its many imitators:

> The *demonization* of a great religious tradition due to the *perverted* actions of a minority of *dissident and distorted voices* remains the real threat, a threat that not only impacts on relations between the Muslim world and the West but also upon growing Muslim populations in the West (1999 [1992], xiii; my italics).

Normative Islam has become something that many, especially in the post-9/11 world, have been quick to define. While perhaps a noble and perhaps even necessary endeavor, it is first and foremost a theological one (i.e., "x" is orthodox; "y" and "z" are heterodox). Moreover, it is a quest that should not concern the professional religionist at all; his or her goal, on the contrary, is to examine how groups legitimate themselves by appealing to ideologies that have historically been constructed and construed as emanating from the divine world. In this construction of identity and the quest for legitimacy, groups such as al-Qaeda and Hamas are certainly no different from any other socio-historical group that defines itself in the light of sources assumed to be divine.

Esposito, like many before him, invokes the trope of religions *qua* vessels of stability and uniformity. This uniformity arises from the inner faith experience (and it is usually in the singular) of practitioners that can take different manifestations in various historical moments:

> For Muslims throughout the centuries, the message of the Quran and the example of the Prophet Muhammad have constituted the formative and enduring foundation of faith and belief. They have served as the basic sources of Islamic law and the reference point for daily life. Muslims today, as in the past, continue to affirm that the Quran is the literal word of God, the Creator's immutable guidance for an otherwise transient world. *This transhistorical significance is rooted in the belief that the Book and the Prophet provide eternal principles and norms on which Muslim life, both individual and collective, is to be patterned. The challenge for each generation of believers has been the continued formulation, appropriation, and implementation of Islam in history* (2005 [1988], 31; my italics).

As we have seen many times before, faith and experience are assumed to provide a stability that grounds the vagaries and instabilities of various historical, social, and cultural forms. This perceived stability of Islam, "epitomized by a common profession of faith and acceptance of the Shari'a, Islamic law" (Esposito 2005 [1988], 66), is what brings coherence to an otherwise disparate collection of data. This is, of course, a chimera. One cannot make appeals to inner experiences, which are inherently unverifiable, to explain a historical, social, or cultural record. One cannot, in other words, define the known by appeals to the unknown. Yet, time and again, appeals to such metaphysics have dictated the study of both religion in general and Islam in particular.

If, on the level of theory, such metaphysical claims are untenable, the practical cost is that they influence the ways in which the readership of such books think about both religion and Islam. What possible intellectual benefit is there to equating faith with some amorphous stability that eludes the inherent instability of history? Genealogically, of course, the moorings of this assumption are in Schleiermacher's attempt to carve out a niche for experience in light of Kantian critiques of the noumenal (Proudfoot 1985, 211–12). This defense, as others have well shown (e.g., Scharf 1999; McCutcheon 1997; Fitzgerald 2000), has entered the critical discourse of religious studies where it is no longer seen as a coping mechanism against a shrinking metaphysical cosmos, but where it is often regarded as *de rigeur*, a fact that it is assumed adequately explains religion and religious phenomena.

This reinforces my point, if indeed it needs reinforcing, that the majority of books that introduce Islam are geared more for an ecumenical or liberal Protestant audience than they are for introductory courses devoted to the academic study of religion. This Islam is not something that is messy or unquantifiable; rather it is, to use the words of McCutcheon, "politically ineffectual and reserved only for some posited interior, personal struggle of faith" (2005, 63). This gives way to the rhetoric of extremists "hijacking the tradition," a trope that I shall explore in greater detail in the following chapter. Esposito, again invoking the stability of a normative Islamic tradition and the movement of extremists beyond its pale, writes that:

> Terrorists such as Osama bin Laden and others *have gone beyond* classical Islam's criteria for a just war. They recognize no limits but their own, employing any weapons or means... At the same time, many *prominent Islamic scholars and religious leaders across the Muslim world have denounced this hijacking of Islam by terrorists*. The Islamic Research Council at al-Azhar University, one of the oldest universities in the world and a leading center of Islamic learning regarded by many as the highest moral authority in Islam, issued strong *authoritative declarations against bin Laden's initiatives* (2005 [1988], 263; my italics).

The discourse that Esposito employs in this passage is surely significant. Mirroring the "hijacking" trope, he creates a scenario that equates bin Laden (and those like him) as innovators, nihilists, people who for various psychological reasons have chosen to depart from, as the title of

Esposito's book makes clear, "the straight path." Juxtaposed against such individuals are the "prominent" scholars at one of the "oldest" universities in not just the Islamic world but also the world at large. These nameless scholars defined by their institutional affiliations as opposed to their charismatic personalities confront, according to the way Esposito sets this up, an individual lacking such credentials. The "authority" of the past thus confronts the initiatives of the "present"; stability, according to this model, must always trump innovation.

Armstrong's *Islam: A Short History*

Karen Armstrong's essentialist reading of Islam has found a large readership in the years following 9/11. Although I am not sure how widespread this book is in college courses devoted to introducing Islam, its general and widespread popular appeal merits its inclusion here. Armstrong, a former nun, attempts to carve out a place for religion deep inside the hearts of believers, a niche where it neither can corrupt nor be corrupted by the external vagaries of history, society, or culture. Indeed, she opens the book with the following "axiom" of the true nature of religion:

> The spiritual quest is an interior journey; it is a psychic rather than a political drama. It is preoccupied with liturgy, doctrine, contemplative disciplines and an *exploration of the heart, not with the clash of current events*...power struggles are not what religion is really about, but an unworthy distraction from the life of the spirit, which is conducted far from the maddening crowd, unseen, silent, and unobtrusive (Armstrong 2000, ix; my italics).[6]

Armstrong subsequently argues, in the name of "the" Hindu tradition, that the historical record is "evanescent, unimportant and insubstantial" (ix). Islam, however, is unique in its ability to deal with and act in history (but surely every religion deals with and acts in history). Falling back on the discourse of divine "kernal" and outer "shell," Armstrong argues that the genius of Islam is its ability to "sacralize" (?) history, to wed a presumably stable and divine essence with the otherwise fractured nature of the exterior life. The genealogy of the inner kernel–outer shell trope, or its alternate faith-based experience versus outer ritual, is an overused one that has its roots in the Protestant assumptions of what true religion is or should be. Perhaps because she is not trained in the critical discourse of religion,[7] Armstrong seems oblivious to her Schleiermachian situatedness. This conception of religion as founded on inner experiences, to use the words of Robert Orsi, has many implications for the ways in which we think about religion and, not surprisingly, it comes with its fair share of distortion:

> True religion, then, is [regarded as] epistemologically and ethically singular. It is rational, respectful of persons, noncoercive, nonanthropomorphic in its higher forms, mystical (as opposed to ritualistic), unmediated and agreeable to democracy (no hierarchy in gilded robes and fancy hats), monotheistic (no angels, saints, demons, ancestors), emotionally controlled, a reality of mind and spirit, not body and matter. It is concerned with ideal essences not actual things, and especially not about presences in things (2005, 188).

These assumptions, like so much of what I have tried to demonstrate in this study, reflect less some natural state than hold up a mirror to the political and ideological assumptions of a particular historical moment. As a number of scholars (e.g., Orsi 2005; Fitzgerald 2000; Wasserstrom 1999) have suggested, all of these closet assumptions about the quiddity of what constitutes religion has led many, especially those with higher degrees in its study, to think that they can somehow make a positive contribution to the betterment of humanity. Whether after the Second World War (cf. Wasserstrom 1999, 30–36) or because of ecumenical concerns (cf. Fitzgerald 2000, 33–37), many scholars of religion buy into an essentialist understanding that facilitates a renewal of religious discourse in the modern world, and the ability of these essentialized religions to talk to one another.

Into this fray we must situate many contemporary scholars of Islam. The scholar of Islamic data who approaches his or her data through social-scientific methodologies or who is interested in the manifold ways that Muslims, geographically and temporally, have constructed truth claims based upon various ideological concerns and the need for legitimization is rare. The need, as the above example shows and as those in the following chapter will as well, to carve out a noumenal Islam of the spirit that is untouched by external events is created by a neat set of rhetorical moves in order to protect what one studies. To reiterate: there is nothing inherently wrong with such an approach; in many instances, it may even be desired. But, to quote from Lincoln's passage that opens up this chapter, it should not "be confused with scholarship" (Lincoln 1996, 227).

Let me return briefly to Armstrong's *Islam: A Short History*. In her concluding chapter to the book, called "Islam Agonistes," she resorts to the fundamentalism-as-perversion trope. For instance, in speaking of the Taliban in Afghanistan, she claims that fundamentalism (of any kind) "perverts the faith and turns it in the *opposite direction of what was intended*" (2000, 17–171; my italics). Again, we see here an expert able to define what constitutes the real form of the religion and, with surgeon-like precision, isolate the carcinogenic tumor perverting its natural functioning.

This biological metaphor is frequently implicit in discussion of the "true" nature of religion and the need to differentiate it from "untrue" ones. Moreover, her comments also work on the assumptions that "religions" actually intend something, itself a problematic claim.

In her conclusion to the volume, Armstrong turns her attention to the events of 9/11. In particular, she writes that:

> However we view American foreign policy, none of this can justify such a murderous attack, which has no sanction in either the Quran or the Shariah... The fear and the rage that lie at the heart of all fundamentalist vision nearly always tend to distort the tradition that fundamentalists are trying to defend, and this has never been more evident than on September 11. *There has seldom been a more flagrant and wicked abuse of religion* (2000, 190; my italics).

There are a number of problems with this passage. First, it is based on the Protestant assumption that everything in a religion must be in "the Book."[8] That is, anything that might distort an original message becomes a later innovation that cannot be justified by the message itself. This, of course, is based on the Protestant critique of Catholicism and, as the quotation from Orsi above demonstrates, is still alive and well in religious studies circles. If the Qur'ān and the Sharī'a do not mention something then it cannot be truly "Islamic." Such an attitude is incorrect because it misses the dynamics of self-legitimacy, not to mention the commentary traditions in medieval and early modern Islam.

Secondly, terms such as "distortion," "flagrant and wicked abuse of religion" are unhelpful. The very term "religion" is so vague and amorphous that one has to ask how could it possibly admit of distortion? Where does this undistorted religion exist? (In the hearts of true believers, of course.) For Armstrong, as for so many others, this discourse of "religion" is so important and urgent because it holds the key to making the world a better place to live. This key or the desire to discover it, however, moves us far beyond the pale of the scholar's workshop.

Denny's *An Introduction to Islam*

One of the most popular books used to introduce undergraduates to Islam in a semester-long course is Frederick Mathewson Denny's *Introduction to Islam*, also now in its third edition. Denny, trained as a historian of religions at the University of Chicago, provides a well-balanced and, for the most part, excellent survey of over 1,400 years of Islamic civilization. Despite this, however, he does gloss over certain key features and, in the process, works with a paradigm of religion that takes much for granted. For example, in his discussion of the Qur'ān, he writes that:

> It is painful for Muslims to witness certain types of historico-critical, philological, and otherwise "Orientalist" scholarly treatment of their sacred book. This reaction can easily be dismissed by outsiders as fundamentalist obscurantism. But much of the modern Western scholarly investigation of the Qur'ān has been a kind of plundering of its contents, to show Semitic parallels, Jewish or Christian origins for the ideas, mistakes in Muhammad's "appropriation" of the senior Abrahamic traditions (thus demonstrating Islam's inferiority because of its lack of originality), and so forth…unsympathetic or historical analyses of the Qur'ān amount to invasions of a Muslim's sense of identity and meaning (Denny 1994, 148).

Here Denny, picking up a thread that I discussed in Chapter 1, adopts the position that "unsympathetic" (?) historical and philological attempts to investigate the origins and contents of the Qur'ān offend Muslim sensibilities. The juxtaposition of "historical account" and "sympathetic" treatment in the above passage are bothersome for a number of reasons. First, it is not the goal of historical accounts or investigations to be sympathetic; the moment it does this it moves out of the realm of scholarship and into that of apologetics and/or theology. Denny, for example, nowhere goes into the details concerning the social-scientific origins of the Qur'ān (e.g., no mention of archaeology, competing inscriptions), which have the potential to illumine greatly the production of early Islamic literature, its competing visions, sites of contestation, etc. What the reader is given, however, is fairly benign treatments about what the Qur'ān means to the Muslim believer, how it is recited, and its liturgical breakdown for the month of Ramadan.

Secondly, it should not matter to the historian or scholar that "historical analyses of the Qur'ān amount to invasions of a Muslim's sense of identity and meaning." If we curtail investigation into certain subjects simply because such investigations might offend some, much of the most important criticism of Western civilization would never have been written. Indeed we would, for example, still be talking of the Hebrew Bible as revealed from Sinai. In terms of religion, this relegates the scholar to the level of color commentator or cheerleader: If one does not or feels that one cannot ask certain questions of one's data then the entire scholarly enterprise breaks down. This certainly is not to claim that scholarship is always objective or that it does not possess wills to power, but self-reflexivity not self-censorship is the way to maneuver around such pitfalls.

Third, and on the level of content, there is no valid scholarly reason to construct hermetically-sealed borders around the Qur'ān. It is a document that was in conversation with Judaism and Christianity, not to mention their respective scriptures. Historical and philological investigations into these conversations provide much needed insights into the nature of how religions think with other religions, why they do so, and how they legitimate themselves in the process. Admittedly, if this is used in the service of showing how Islam is derivative and/or inferior because it is nothing more than a repository of earlier ideas then it has to be realized that this is an equally apologetic claim.

Denny's brief comments cited above, then, accurately mirror the current state of affairs in Islamic studies. Very few are willing to write about Islamic origins, and there is a tendency to do precisely what Denny does: gravitate towards soft or innocuous themes, such as Quranic recitation or a quasi-theological explanation of certain themes in the book itself (e.g., Rahman 1980; Sells 1999). This self-censorship or unwillingness to ask hard questions of Islamic data and instead offer sympathetic readings of such data is, as far as I am concerned, one of the biggest obstacles currently facing the *academic* study of Islam.

When it comes to modern Islam, however, Denny is often much more nuanced than others discussed in this chapter. He acknowledges, for example, that contemporary Islam is a "vigorous, complex amalgam of peoples, movements, and not the monolithic, centrally coordinated, hostile enterprise that outsiders sometimes assume it to be" (1994, 345). He is not nearly as essentialist in his understanding of the tradition as those witnessed above. Denny does not, for example, implicitly fall back on the essence-manifestations, inner faith–outer distortion.

Yet, as I argued above, the real shortcoming of Denny's book is its unwillingness to move beyond understanding. This term, genealogically emerging from *Verstehen*, is a technical one that implies that there is something that can appropriately be labeled as religious, and that the historian of religion possesses the unique tools to uncover it. As Preus and others would argue, the desire to understand as opposed to explain is not necessarily helpful to the professional religionist.

Within this context, Denny is uninterested in proffering explanations of Islamic data that swerve too far from the way Muslims themselves would understand such data. We saw this above in his "analysis" of the Qur'ān, and we witness it again in his understanding of modern Islam. For example, he writes of "Islamic fundamentalism" that:

> Our preference is to avoid characterizing Muslims as fundamentalists whenever possible and instead, to treat movements and schools case by case. Fundamentalism as a term too often serves as a negative label obscuring what we are *trying to understand and appreciate*… And the frequent association of the term (especially in the media) with terrorism, backwardness, "medieval" mentality, and general closed-mindedness may reveal more about the people using the term than its referent(s) (1994, 347; my italics).

Here Denny rejects the conceptual framework of the "comparative religionist" that seeks to isolate a cross-cultural phenomenon that desires to return to the "fundamentals" of a tradition, real or perceived. In its place, he moves into a case-by-case explanation of various Islamic "reform" movements. Although he provides good thick descriptions of these movements, they are nothing more than descriptions. For example, Denny gives us a detailed description of Sayyid Qutb, a leading member of the Muslim Brotherhood in Egypt: He provides background on Qutb, his travels and disillusionment in America, what he wrote, that he was executed by the Egyptian authorities in 1966, and that his writings influence many Muslims, including those in North America. And that is it. Denny makes no mention of the ideology of Islamic reform in general or of Sayyid Qutb in particular. How, for example, does Qutb make Islam in his own image? What does he use to legitimate his case? Why? How come Qutb's vision plays such a large role in shaping groups like al-Qaeda? Rather than provide us with any kind of explanation, Denny provides us with *Verstehen*, understanding, and little else. (For a much more provocative and stimulating analysis of Qutb, see Lincoln 2003, 3–5, 14–16.)

This chapter has attempted to show the apologetic foundation upon which the edifice of Islamic studies currently rests. It did this by analyzing how Islam is introduced to both undergraduates and the general reading public. In particular, the argument was that such presentations are neither innocent, coincidental, nor objective. On the contrary, such presentations are based on a crypto-theological set of assumptions, ones that lurk furtively within the halls of religious studies and ones that all too frequently make their way into discussions about the nature of religion in general and Islam (or other specific religions) in particular. This Islam (always in the singular) of the spirit, as I intimated here and will flesh out in the chapters that follow, is completely out of sync with current *critical discourses* produced by certain voices within religious studies. In many ways it is easy to fall back upon this Islam of the spirit in the current political moment, one in which Muslims are constantly regarded as having a propensity towards any number of values that are seen as hostile to ours or the West. Although the reasons for such constructions are perhaps transparent, their application to create an overarching discourse of Islamic studies, one to which practitioners must subscribe to be considered part of the in group, is certainly not. Specialists in Islam, I contend, must begin to gravitate towards the critical discourses of religious studies and other disciplines and, in so doing, move away from the assumption that data neatly and naturally exist in the world. Only such a movement will insure the survival of the field at the current hostile moment, in addition to paving the way for important research in the future.

5 The Implosion of a Discipline: 9/11 and the Islamic Studies Scholar as Media Expert

> Well, I fin'ly started thinking straight
> When I run out of things to investigate
> Couldn't imagine doing anything else
> So now I'm sitting home investigatin' myself!
> Hope I don't find out anything…hmm great God![1] (Bob Dylan)

The discipline of Islamic studies has been effortlessly coasting in essentialist mode, happily subscribing to the nostalgia of authenticity and the touchstone of inner experience. This, despite several persuasive critiques mounted internally within religious studies to interrogate the genealogies and categorical assumptions to which the field has traditionally ascribed, and to which it continues to do so. Although this interrogation made little if no impact on the study of Islam, another event, one uncanny and not academic in the slightest, would create a sea-change in the ways that Islamicists perceived themselves and were perceived by others, not only inside the academy but also outside of it. The events of September 11, 2001, witnessed the transformation of many Islamicists from being specialists in often-arcane areas of medieval Islamic jurisprudence or philosophy to sudden experts in Islamic mentalities (a genealogy that should not come as a surprise given the subject matter of Chapter 2). As the media came calling, many Islamicists were hauled (often all too happily) in front of cameras to inform an ignorant public about the eternal truths of Islam and to establish the fact that those who perpetrated the attacks of 9/11 were not real Muslims. Questions of the day included "Why do they hate us so much?" (answer: they don't); "What kind of religion would commit such atrocities?" (answer: a religion hijacked by terrorists). Afraid that their life's work was under attack, many Islamicists were all too willing to defend Islam, at whatever cost, against a hostile and unsympathetic American public.

The present chapter examines the repercussions of a major world event on an academic discipline. How does the "religious studies" expert handle oneself when perpetuators of a horrible event claim to act in the name of religion in general, and that of the religion in which one specializes in particular? Into what sorts of situations or contortions have the events of

9/11 put the professional Islamicist? Although area studies experts had long been called upon by the media and various think tanks to comment on the Cold War, this was usually done in the name of a region or a specific country; rarely if ever did religion figure highly in such discussion. Social science, it will be recalled from Chapter 2, always trumped the humanities. Now, however, the focus is put on religion, that highly murky and amorphous concept that, at one and the same time, is both everywhere and nowhere. This created all sorts of problems for Islamicists, especially those not grounded in the critical discourses of the larger discipline. How, for example, can one speak about religion, let alone a religion, using the sound bites afforded by the media? The nuance of the scholar's workshop had to give way quickly to the essences demanded by the public. My claim in this chapter is that because Islamic studies has always been theoretically unsophisticated, those specializing in it were simply unable to rise to the challenge. Although there is nothing inherently wrong with wanting to convince people that all Muslims were not complicit in events such as 9/11, something that should be obvious to anyone, the job of the ideal religionist is not to apologize, but to contextualize, to explain, to theorize, all of which involves moving beyond the essentialisms to which generic terms such as religion and Islam have unfortunately habituated us.

The results, however, have not been pretty. Virtually overnight, Islamic studies went from a discipline with a considerable amount of historical (though not necessarily critical) depth to one that was interested almost solely in explaining why Muslims were not the "bad guys." This is not to imply that this is wrong. It is a scholar's natural reaction to want to defend his or her object of study from distortion and overtly prejudicial stereotyping. The various involvements with the media, church groups, inter-faith meetings, and campus lectures have all played an important role in helping to shape positively the opinions of certain segments of the American public.

Yet whenever one has to defend something publicly, using various media that do not generally admit of nuance or shades of grey, distortion inevitably sets in. Unfortunately, in the present case this has resulted in many Islamicists resorting to the most unfortunate essentialisms in order to protect a perceived kernel that is regarded as somehow definitive of something called Islam. Rather than talk about the skirmishes of regimes of truth that the generic term religion often masks, we are frequently left with insipid slogans such as the equation of islam with peace (*salām*) since both have the same root, *s-l-m* (e.g., Ayoub 2002, 341). If this were not bad enough, many often employed outmoded theories of religion, ones that were often premised on binary oppositions, such as that between orthodox/heterodox (see the informative discussion of this genealogy in Dubuisson 2003, 103–106). This most frequently took the form of claiming that the perpetrators of such acts could not really have been "Muslims" because something monolithically known as Islam does not condone terrorism.

Missing in all of these statements of course is the critical discourses devoted to understanding the manifold ways in which ideology masquerades as religion. Very few scholars of Islam question the guiding assumption that there exists some *sui generis* phenomenon known as religion. Rarely are Islamicists willing to entertain replacing religion with ideology, a shifting and dynamic discourse that is not essential, but a site, or perhaps better a series of sites, of skirmishes, of competing truth claims. The so-called discipline of religious studies, despite claims to the contrary, does not provide some sort of Archimedean fulcrum point with which to understand the world's religions; rather, it too becomes one more set of ideologies complicit in the manufacture of other ideologies, a series of processes to which the discipline unhelpfully gives the name religion or religions.

In what follows, my goal is to survey and analyze some of the many statements issued by professional Islamicists in the aftermath of 9/11. Many of these statements, whether issued publicly or in more popular monographs, further contribute to the sad state of affairs currently plaguing the academic study of Islam. The overwhelming majority of such statements are not new; on the contrary, they emerge out of the various genealogical trajectories that I examined in previous chapters. What is new, however, is the intensity. Although before such essentialist statements appeared in academic monographs with considerable frequency, we now witness the wholesale adoption of this model in print and public, academic and non-academic settings. It is a discourse that appears at conferences (where we witness panels on "Progressive Muslims," to be discussed below), in the media, and in monographs meant for both popular and academic consumption.

The Immediate Aftermath: Islamicists Respond

As I mentioned above, the days immediately following 9/11 witnessed an unprecedented attack on Islam in the media.[2] I should be clear here: from the perspective of service or maintaining civic peace, there is absolutely nothing wrong with coming to the defense of a religion. In fact, it is something that was probably necessary. However, I do have problems when this defense is carried out using the mantle of the discipline of religious studies or Islamic studies, the job of which is ideally to complicate rather than to essentialize. Given the fact that the media by nature is not particularly prone to nuance, perhaps the various ways in which professional Islamicists responded to its queries could not have been otherwise. When one is on the defensive to speak for a civilization that is being misrepresented by intentional metonymic slippages, it is not always easy to overcomplicate things. After such a traumatic event, something that many believed was endorsed by a monolithic entity known as Islam, people wanted answers.

Yet despite the hostile attacks and the media onslaught, the subsequent desire to defend at all costs something problematically defined as a normative Islam, one that just happened to mirror the democratic and liberal values of the West (see the discussion in McCutcheon 2005, 47–62), has had many unintended consequences and will continue to have them. Moreover, as I tried to demonstrate in the previous chapter, this discourse of creating such an "Islam" and then holding it up to examine the orthodox or heterodox nature of other islams is certainly not new. On the contrary, although it has been going on since the Cold War, it was a discourse that only intensified when Islamicists picked up the *sui generis* slogan of religionists in the 1970s and 1980s.

An Islamicist who defends a constructed normative Islam in the media might well be forgiven if he or she complexly nuanced Islamic data in his or her own academic writings. Unfortunately, as I have argued throughout, this is something that is rarely done. Scholars do not just suddenly pick up an essentialist and essentializing discourse from nowhere in order to confront the media; it has to be there to begin with. In other words, one falls back on it; one does not create it ex *nihilo*. It is precisely this genealogy that has, in many ways, taken over the discipline, masquerading as the way to study Islam as opposed to being understood as but one genealogy among competing genealogies. The essentialism that I examined in the previous two chapters that stressed the rhetoric of faith and the authenticity of inner experiences that move uncontested and effortlessly through history, shaping various historical moments and geographical areas, is implicit in the baggage that Islamic studies carries. As a consequence, this discourse became all too easy to rely upon and to invoke with pre-packaged slogans in the aftermath of 9/11.

Looked at from the other side, that of critical discourses and the ideology or rhetorics of disciplinary formations, the parroting of essentialist slogans tends to circle back and re-enter into the academic discourse in whose name it proposes to speak. My concern here is that Islamicists have been put in such a defensive position that it might very well be difficult to emerge unscathed at the end of the process. The political fight to defend a normative Islam and normative Muslims, as if such phenomena have ever existed or could ever exist, will have negative repercussions on the future of the field from which it will be very difficult to escape.

Within this context, and I certainly learned this from my own work with the media after 9/11, it is all too easy to fall back upon essentialisms when confronted by a hostile media or audience. How is one supposed to respond when angry members of an audience demand to know why Muslims flew into the World Trade Center and the Pentagon? One can certainly say that they were not real Muslims, conveniently side-stepping the issue, but the fact remains that the perpetrators certainly considered themselves to be not only real, but the most authentic Muslims (cf. the letter of Muhammad Atta produced in Lincoln 2003, 93–98). On one level, then, Islamicists can speak ad nauseum about avoiding essentialisms and the manner in which Islam, like other religions, witnesses various struggles for authority and legitimation. But by this point everyone's eyes have glazed over and they are no longer listening to us. Or, if one does something with the media, these comments are usually removed or glossed over.

It also becomes increasingly difficult, unless of course we follow the Wilfred Cantwell Smith model, to be a spokesperson for those we study. Since many Muslims were afraid to defend publicly a normative Islam that could not or would not endorse such violent acts, professional Islamicists became all too willing to engage in this sort of activity. If all we, as professional Islamicists, can say about Muslims is that which they themselves would be comfortable with or that wind up being so innocuous that we produce meaningless essentialisms and generalizations then we have largely failed to do our job. Muslims do kill in the name of religion (just as Jews, Christians, Buddhists, and others do). Our goal must not be to convince others, in the name of liberal democracy or some form of Protestant ecumenism, that we can all just get along if we better understand each other. According to McCutcheon, "our role as scholars ought not to be that of nurturing identification with our objects of study through entering a dialogue with them about our deepest dreams and our ultimate concerns" (2005, 28).

Our goal, then, is not to make selections on what to include in some master narrative based on the criteria of that which bothers us or that which estranges us (Lincoln 1989, 10). If we do this and sweep all else under a hermeneutical carpet then we end up doing little more than providing color commentary to that which others tell themselves and ultimately convince themselves that by retelling it enough times it must be part of the natural order of things.

A pertinent example comes from the official response to the 9/11 attacks issued by the "Steering Committee and Members, Section of the Study of Islam." Implicit in the statement is precisely the essentialism that I have highlighted time and again throughout the previous chapters. In particular:

> As scholars of religious traditions, we observe that religious symbols are used for political motives all over the world in Hindu, Christian, Jewish, and Muslim traditions. However, *we must critically distinguish between politically motivated deployment of religious symbols and the highest ideals that these traditions embody. Just as most would regard bombers of abortion clinics to be outside the pale of Christianity, so the actions of these terrorists should not be accepted as representing Islam in any way* (http://groups.colgate.edu/aarislam/sois.htm; my italics).

Here we see clearly the naïve, if not impossible, juxtaposition of the political and the "highest" (presumably a buzzword for religious and hence true and real) uses of so-called religious symbols, whatever these may be. There exists here neither the sense nor the desire to talk about the ways in which religions are constructed, the ways in which they represent the sublimation of human discourses, the way that, to use the words of Lincoln, religious discourses "recode virtually any content as sacred, ranging from the high-minded and progressive to the murderous, oppressive, and banal" (Lincoln 2003, 6).

Moreover, the above statement also works on the assumption that there exists a normative tradition that has somehow been hijacked by extremists. Terrorism, in other words, is juxtaposed here with a true representation of Islam. Real Muslims could never commit such atrocious acts because such acts somehow run antithetical to what real religion should be or is constructed to be (i.e., apolitical, peaceful, based on inner experiences). All of this despite the fact that the perpetrators of the acts saw themselves as the only true Muslims, those unwilling to acquiesce to the forces of western imperialism, and so on. What we see here is the reversal of the Cantwell Smithian approach, and it is invoked for no other reason than that it becomes intellectually convenient. In other words, it is acceptable to describe others in ways that suit them when that description neatly fits or coincides with our own construction of what or how those others should be. Yet, when it is inconvenient such descriptions must be modified and a hermeneutic of suspicion applied to the group or groups that threaten our taxonomies.

As if to give this highly problematic statement an air of truth or authenticity a comparative dimension is added (perhaps an attempt to invoke

5 The Implosion of a Discipline

Müller's trademark phrasing that "to know one is to know none"). Just as the terrorists who committed the acts of 9/11 were not true Muslims, those who bomb abortion clinics in the name of Christianity cannot and must not be *real* Christians. This statement and those who penned it thus buy into a discourse that only that which is allowed to count as truly religious or authentically pious are those beliefs (and often not necessarily actions) that are apolitical and motivated from the murky realms of experience, the so-called inner struggle of faith. This construction of religion is not about reflecting the quirkinesses of human behavior, but about mapping amorphous ideal essences in some metaphysical cartography.

To me, the aforementioned statement is so problematic precisely because it is issued by professional religionists, the main institutional body representing *scholars working in the twin fields of Islam and religious studies*! This is why it is worth repeating that a momentous event such as 9/11 has had tremendous repercussions on the development of a field of research. Virtually overnight scholars engaged in and doing good work in various areas of Islamic cultures became involved in the media, where they were reduced to relying upon and ultimately parroting all sorts of ridiculous essentialisms. Presumably this was done in order to protect an object of study held dear; however this, to use the words of Lincoln that I have invoked frequently throughout this study, "should not be confused with scholarship" (Lincoln 1996, 227).

Within this context, it is worth pointing out the opposite academic reaction to the events of 9/11. This reaction tended to come from the direction of so-called "neo-conservatives," i.e., those often actively involved in foreign policy initiatives within the Bush administration. Invoking Chapter 2 above, these individuals have their own genealogical baggage, most of which stems form the Cold War desire to understand a region and, in the process, to be able to predict what it can or cannot do. Again, to show that the study of Islam in North America does not really change or develop new paradigms, those scholars in this so-called "neo-con" camp are primarily influenced by Bernard Lewis and are often highly critical of professional Islamicists who, in their opinion, rely far too heavily on the writings of Edward Said. Very little, in other words, has changed since the clash of paradigms that I highlighted in the first chapter of this study.

Because of spatial restraints, let me focus briefly here on Martin Kramer's influential (at least in certain corridors) *Ivory Towers on Sand*, published by the Washington Institute for Near East Policy in the immediate aftermath of 9/11. The work itself is better contextualized by its subtitle: *The Failure of Middle Eastern Studies in America*. This book amounts to a stinging indictment of the field of Middle Eastern studies, especially the inability of its so-called experts to engage objectively the political situation of the contemporary Middle East. Kramer is particularly critical of the Saidian influence on a field that, in his opinion, has created a generation of apologists who misread the threat of Islamism and civil society especially in the Arab World.

Perhaps not coincidentally Kramer is an American who for years ran the Moshe Dayan Center for Middle Eastern and African Studies at Tel Aviv University. The fact that Kramer spent years in Israel (and presumably is also an Israeli citizen) does not automatically mean that we should write him off, as many Islamicists in the field did after the publication of his book. That Kramer spent so long in Israel, however, certainly helps to situate his take on Middle Eastern politics, especially the desired ability to predict unrest on the Arab "street" and the importance of security from terrorist attacks, two features that are extremely important to the state of Israel and, by extension, many Israelis working in the field of contemporary politics in an often extremely volatile region.

Like all books that go over the top in their criticisms, however, there is often much of validity to be found within. Yet, owing to the sarcastic tone and highly polemical tenor of his work, Kramer rubbed many people up the wrong way. I have discussed some of the validities in Kramer's research in previous chapters; my goal here, on the contrary, is to demonstrate that his thesis, although not without merits, is as much a reaction to the events of 9/11 as the equally problematic assumptions of those working in the field of Islamic studies. For Kramer, the field of Middle Eastern studies, much like Adams's religious studies, has not lived up to its promise. Yet unlike Adams who would assign all the blame squarely on the shoulders of religious studies, Kramer faults the disciplinary conformity, itself based on the construction of false icons (e.g., Said) to which scholars must genuflect if they are to advance their careers in "the guild" (2001, 3).

In the introduction to the book, Kramer expresses his dissatisfaction with the self-confidence of so-called experts of the Middle East, many of whom pride themselves on their competency and ability to understand this region and predict future developments. According to him, only in the aftermath of 9/11

> have hesitant voices been raised from within the ramparts, pointing to serious problems. They run even deeper than insiders are prepared to admit. It is no exaggeration to say that America's academics have failed to predict or explain the major evolutions of Middle Eastern politics and society over the past two decades. Time and again, academics have been taken by surprise by their subjects; time and again, their paradigms have been swept by events. Repeated failures have depleted the credibility of scholarship among influential publics. In

5 The Implosion of a Discipline

Washington, the mere mention of academic Middle Eastern studies often causes eyes to roll. The purpose of this paper is to probe how and why a branch of academe once regarded with esteem has descended to such a low point in the public estimate, and what might be done about it (2001, 2).

Here Kramer, I think mistakenly, defines the field's validity or *raison d'être* as the ability to predict events in the Middle East (e.g., the Iranian revolution, first and second intifadas, the rise and influence of al-Qaeda, 9/11). Perhaps (but again I am not entirely convinced) this is the goal of those working on Islamic political systems in political science departments, but certainly not what should define those working in history, religious studies, sociology and other departments. Moreover, just because someone working in Islamic politics does not accurately predict an event such as 9/11 does not necessarily mean that he or she is unqualified to be an expert in the Middle East or that he or she is somehow unaware of the hostility against American foreign policy on the so-called Arab street. Perhaps the biggest argument against the prognosticative quality that Kramer so desires is the universal condemnation and predictions of chaos concerning the recent American invasion of Iraq on the part of experts, be they in Middle Eastern studies or Islamic studies. Despite such predictions, the American government, under the influence of neo-cons, still decided to invade.

Kramer, however, would take this consensus of American Middle East experts against the Iraq invasion as further evidence for failure. For him, the objections of such experts resides less in their ability to prognosticate than in their dangerous identification with the Islamic world. This identification has created a scenario in which experts on Islam and the Middle East are clouded by sympathy to the Arab world, and often concomitant hostility to Israel, which they lump together with American foreign policy. Such sympathies, Kramer argues, makes them far from impartial or objective observers of contemporary events (2001, 44–57). The figure most responsible for this identification, according to Kramer, is Edward Said:

> *Orientalism* made it acceptable, even expected, for scholars to spell out their own political commitments as a preface to anything they wrote or did. More than that, it also enshrined an acceptable hierarchy of political commitments, with Palestine at the top, followed by the Arab nation and the Islamic world. They were the long-suffering victims of Western racism, American imperialism, and Israeli Zionism – the three legs of the Orientalist stool (2001, 37).

This political identification of Middle Eastern and Islamic experts with Palestinian and other causes, for Kramer, has both blindfolded and hamstrung the discipline. According to him, many experts in the Middle East and Islam tend to regard the actions by Islamists, including terrorist activity, as nothing more than responses to American-Israeli aggression. Rather than criticize such actions there is a tendency, as I suggested above, to write them off as non-essential to Islam or, according to Kramer, "another opportunity for the repetitive and ritual denunciation of Western prejudice against Islam" (2001, 45).

To rectify the situation, Kramer calls for a massive rethinking of the field. One of the first things that he calls for is a review of Title VI, the federal program, discussed above in Chapter 2, responsible for funding area studies programs. Such a review, he contends, would "sensitize the academic recipients of taxpayer dollars to the concerns of the American people, expressed through their elected representatives" (2001, 129). Such a review, *inter alia*, Kramer argues will go a long way to reinventing the field of Middle Eastern studies. He concludes his study by arguing that changes such as these will subsequently lead to understanding

> that which is uniquely American in the American approach to the Middle East. The idea that the United States plays an essentially beneficent role in the world is at the very core of this approach. So is a willingness to constructively engage one's own government and fellow citizens. This willingness need not imply the neglect of pure scholarship, a narrow nationalism, or even a renunciation of all Middle Eastern preferences. But it does imply that the scholar has a constituency outside the campus gates that deserves to be addressed (2001, 129).

There are certainly a number of problematic assumptions in this passage. Not the least of which is that the United States, and its foreign policy initiatives, is an agent of beneficence throughout the world! Moreover, the claim that the scholar of the Middle East or Islam is somehow responsible to a constituency "outside the campus gates" is not entirely clear. Who is this constituency? The government? Those who support the government? What about all those American constituencies that are increasingly critical of the government? Surely the goal of scholarship is not simply to provide tacit endorsement to a partisan government that is looking for political justification to legitimate certain actions in the Middle East. Kramer, then, calls for a return to Cold War policy. In this regard, I need very little other support for my argument that there is nothing new here. Kramer and his allies, on the one hand, versus Near Eastern specialists on the other is little more than a replay of the Lewis–Said debates that I used as an anecdote to begin this study in Chapter 1. The situation of Islam is not moving forward, but is caught endlessly in the past.

Kramer's critiques have been highly influential in the corridors of power in Washington, and, in many ways, they have the potential to be highly devastating to the future of the field's funding. *Ivory Towers on Sand* received a significant amount of attention in the mainstream media (including the *Washington Post* and the *New York Times*). Kramer's

5 The Implosion of a Discipline

arguments became the driving force behind numerous critical articles on the field of Middle Eastern studies and its main institutional voice, Middle East Studies Association (MESA), in such magazines as the *National Review, Commentary* and the *New Republic*. To demonstrate to just what extent Kramer's ideas trickled down into the more popular media, consider the following comments by Stanley Kurtz, a conservative journalist for the *National Review*:

> To discover the truth about the Middle East, students need to be able to compare competing perspectives – those of Said and Lewis... The unfortunate truth, however, is that the followers of Bernard Lewis have largely been banned from college campuses by the followers of Edward Said. And Said's followers have done so because they adhere to a postmodern view that specifically rejects the premises of John Stuart Mill's liberalism. In the view of Said and his followers, ideas are not merely competing truths that we can accept or reject, but masks for oppressive power. In this view (derived from Karl Marx via Michel Foucault), to allow ideas to compete freely in the marketplace is to license oppression... Of course, when their political-ideological monopoly is challenged, the denizens of the postmodern academy quickly revert to liberal principles to defend themselves from the supposed "censorship" of their opponents. This is bad faith. The postmodern professorate has already destroyed free speech and academic freedom by killing off the marketplace of ideas. On top of that, these professors have the nerve to demand that the federal government subsidize their ideological monopoly to the tune of millions of dollars. Somehow a simple call for viewpoint diversity – the one kind of diversity colleges really ought to be in the business of promoting – is treated as censorship (Kurtz 2003).

The mainstream media has the ability to motivate their larger readerships to lobby Congress in ways that might well impact the field. In June 2003, for example, the Select Education Subcommittee of the House Committee on Education and the Workforce convened brief hearings on "International Programs in Higher Education and Questions of Bias" (Lockman 2004b). The bill emerging from this subcommittee, HR 3077, would provide for the establishment of a so-called International Higher Education Advisory Board with the power to "monitor, apprise and evaluate a sample of activities supported under [Title VI] in order to provide recommendations to the Secretary and the Congress for the improvement of programs under the title and to ensure programs meet the purposes of the title" (quoted in Lockman 2004b). Of the members appointed to this Board, more than half of the members (i.e., four) would be Congressional appointees, and another two would be represented by government agencies concerned with national security (Lockman 2004b).

Another fallout from Kramer's *Ivory Towers on Sand* is the organization entitled "Campus Watch." The goal of this organization, developed and run by Daniel Pipes, also associated with the so-called "neo-con" movement, is to publish, according to its website,

> reviews and critiques of Middle East studies in North America, with an aim to improving them. The project mainly addresses five problems: analytical failures, the mixing of politics with scholarship, intolerance of alternative views, apologetics, and the abuse of power over students. Campus Watch fully respects the freedom of speech of those it debates while insisting on its own freedom to comment on their words and deeds (http://www.campus-watch.org/about.php).

On this website readers can read a "survey of institutions," in which various Middle Eastern studies programs are rated and commented upon based on the way they, or at least those teaching in them, fall on the Middle East divide (i.e., pro-Palestinian or pro-Israeli). Another section, entitled "Keep Us Informed," allows students or other parties with vested interests to keep the organizers of Campus Watch informed about goings on at their local universities:

> Please fill out and submit this page to provide Campus Watch with reports on Middle East-related scholarship, lectures, classes, demonstrations, and other activities relevant to Campus Watch. Information not yet published or only reported in the local/campus press is most useful to us. And don't assume the information need be negative; we are very interested in learning about professors and administrators who do credit to Middle East studies (http://www.campus-watch.org/incident.php).

It is certainly important to be aware of organizations such as Campus Watch if for no other reason than to lend credence to my main argument that the construction and situation of Islam is (and has always been) a highly political endeavor. However, to focus too much time and energy on such organizations, whether pro or con, is not helpful and removes us from the tenor of this chapter. The lists of problematic professors of Middle Eastern and Islamic studies, the various programs that come across as pro-Palestinian, pro-Arab or pro-Israel, students (Arab, Muslim or Jewish) that feel they are being coerced to hold certain views in a classroom although problematic from an intellectual perspective, are not nor should not necessarily be front page news on conservative magazines, inside stories in the *New York Times*, or subjects of congressional subcommittees.

Perhaps a fitting way to end this section is to say that the many problems caused by the study of Islam and the Middle East, problems that this study has traced from Abraham Geiger in the nineteenth century, are not going to go away any time soon. The representation of any religion is fraught with assumptions, presuppositions, and wills to power. In this respect Islam is certainly no different than, say, Buddhism or Hinduism. However, what makes the representations of Islam much different is the manner in which Islam is currently embedded in the popular and governmental imaginations. Experts in Islam are constantly held under governmental scrutiny with the threat of withholding funds that keep their centers, programs, and language studies training afloat. Self-styled conservative watchdogs such as Campus Watch or Jihad Watch monitor the actions of experts in Islam and the Middle East for bias. Meanwhile we are still stuck in the Said–Lewis exchange from over twenty-five years ago. Surely someone has something new to say on all this.

The Response of Islamicists

Those Islamicists who happen to work in the field of what many would call religious studies responded not so much to Kramer's attacks, but to those of militants who would claim to speak in the name of some normative Islam. Once again, unless it should come as a surprise to anyone, such appeals were firmly grounded in essentialism (e.g., Islam is "a, b, and c"; but not "x, y, and z"). In this section I shall survey, very briefly, two books written by well-known Islamicists that engage in precisely this type of essentializing. The two books are Seyyed Hossein Nasr's *The Heart of Islam: Enduring Values for Humanity* (2002), and John Esposito's *Unholy War: Terror in the Name of Islam* (2003). These two monographs, both of which wear their hearts unceremoniously on their book sleeves, attempt, as their titles suggest, not only to clarify a noumenal Islam, but to show how, in the case of Esposito, all who commit violence or terror in the name of Islam are somehow "unholy"; and, in the case of Nasr, that the essence (= "heart") of Islam has something spiritual to teach all of humanity.

Nasr, according to the Seyyed Hossein Nasr Foundation webpage, is University Professor of Islamic studies in the department of religion at George Washington University. The goal of his foundation, as the website makes clear, is

> to propagate traditional teachings, in general, and the various facets of *traditional Islam* and other religions, in particular. Spiritually located in the *perennial philosophy*, traditional teachings are reflected not only religious teachings [sic] but also in philosophy, the sciences and arts. With special emphasis on manifesting these perennial teachings as contained in the *Quran*, the Foundation will include studies on the various facets of Islamic thought, art and civilization (http://www.nasrfoundation.org/aims.html; his italics).

The emphases on "traditional Islam," "spirituality," and "perennial philosophy" automatically situates Nasr within a particular discourse. One can, of course, only speak of a tradition or the traditional in times of turmoil or social disruption at which point it can conveniently be put into counterpoint with something marked as that which is "un-traditional" (Hobsbawm 1992, 2–4; Hughes 2005, 53–54). Tradition, in other words, is an invention, something with a distinctly modern provenance, something that cannot be neatly separated from manifold political and ideological contexts. Likewise, the term "spirituality" is also one that is distinctly modern and that comes out of a particular genealogy or way of thinking about religion (see the discussion in Scharf 1999; Proudfoot 1985, 119–36). "Perennial philosophy," that tradition of wisdom that is thought to course through the veins of the world's religions – irrespective of historical, ideological, or geographic circumstances – is, like traditional and spirituality, not an innocent term that reflects the natural workings of the world, but is a particular discourse that emerged at a particular moment to safeguard religion from, to use the words of Schleiermacher, its various cultured despisers.

In other words, Nasr's website, like much of his scholarly writings, is meant to come across as an accurate description of something called "Islam." In fact, like all writings (academic or otherwise), it is reducible to a number of assumptions, what Lincoln calls "mythology with footnotes" (1999, 209) – although, in the case of *The Heart of Islam*, there are, quite literally, no footnotes. In the preface to the work, Nasr is quick to dismiss all those Orientalists who are "rationalist, historic and skeptical" (2002, xii) of spirituality and religion in general and Islam in particular. In juxtaposition to this, he provides his own brief "historiography" of the field:

> It was not until the second half of the twentieth century that born Muslims well versed in Western languages and methods of research began to write in-depth works on Islam in European languages to explain the tradition in a serious way to the Western audience. They were joined in this task by a number of Western intellectual and spiritual figures and scholars who had been able to penetrate the Islamic universe of meaning and to speak and write from within the Islamic tradition. *As a result of the effort of these two groups, a number of authentic and profound books on various aspects of Islam appeared in English and other European languages* (2002, xii–xiii; my italics).

Here Nasr, like so many, works on the assumption that the principle that guides studying and writing on religion is accuracy. That is, the scholar of Islam is judged credible or not by his or her ability to "speak and write from within the Islamic tradition." Anyone who does not do this, anyone who applies categories that are at all critical of Islam becomes, in his words, an Orientalist, someone with "the arrogant belief that they possessed a flawless scientific method that applied universally to all religions" (2002, xii). Moreover, the last thing that such scholars are

5 The Implosion of a Discipline

interested in is "what Muslims, or for that matter Hindus or Buddhists, thought about their own religious universe" (2002, xii).

Profundity, at least in Nasr's conception of the term, is not based upon critical scholarship, nor upon the ability to use a discourse that does not take what religious people tell us at face value. In fact, Nasr is by no means alone in this. As the critical comments by the likes of Kramer and others become popular, the reaction of many Islamicists is to seek refuge in the rhetorics of authenticity. Although certain scholars and commentators may be critical of Islam, they do so because they are heirs to Orientalism, and because of this, they do not adequately understand what Nasr calls "the heart of Islam." But this is obfuscation. Just as Schleiermacher tried to carve out space for a murky inner experience in the light of Kant's critique, people like Nasr construct an equally murky or numinous Islam that subsequently becomes the touchstone for something that they refer to as true understanding. Nasr describes this noumenal Islam using the sustained metaphor of a Persian carpet:

> [Islam] has incredible diversity and complexity, yet it is dominated by a unity into which all the complex geometric and arabesque patterns are integrated. This complexity can be better understood if one views it as the superimposition of a number of patterns upon the plane of a carpet. In the vast world of Islam also, one can gain a better grasp of the whole by separating the patterns and seeing how each is related to the vertical and horizontal dimensions of the religion of Islam itself as well as to cultural, ethnic, and linguistic factors...in which unity leads to diversity and diversity is integrated into unity (2002, 57).

Here again we see how little the academic discourse resonating in certain segments of Islamic studies has moved since the time of Cantwell Smith and Hodgson. What would it look like if we took out the essence that is all too easily dubbed Islam? How would our descriptive analyses morph once we removed a vague and stable kernel that practitioners say they adhere to, when in fact the reality is much more complicated? How is the activity of making meaning by appealing to something called Islam different from the passive adoption of its forms? Such questions are never entertained in this literature. Part of the reason for this is, as I highlighted in Chapter 1, that those who ask such questions, especially in the light of Saidian critiques, are marginalized as partisans of Orientalism.

Near the end of *The Heart of Islam*, Nasr concludes in typical fashion by arguing that the solutions facing the current plight must involve understanding the universal truths that support not only Islam, but all religions:

> It is only on the basis of a positive and mutually enriching dialogue between religious traditions that respects particularities as well as recognizes the universal truths lying in the heart or center that the answers must be sought for the most acute problems facing humanity today (2002, 313).

This is a political statement. It turns on the assumption that religions are true just because those who consider themselves to be religious believe they are true. But what happens when one pulls back from such assumptions? What happens when we see religions as nothing more or less than a series of discursive practices, the sites where various rival truth claims confront one another, often violently, for legitimation? Surely it is time for scholars of Islam to move beyond color commentary and into the realm of critical discourses.

Another very popular book written by a professional Islamicist in the aftermath of 9/11 was John Esposito's *Unholy War: Terror in the Name of Islam*. I have already discussed some of the theoretical assumptions about the nature of religion in general and Islam in particular that drive his work in the previous chapter. My goal here is not to add so much to the previous discussion, but again to show the response of professional Islamicists to the events of 9/11. My argument, if indeed it needs repeating, is that as the fascinations of the mainstream media have generally been critical of Islam and as scholars such as Kramer have tried to undermine the viability of the discipline, Islamicists have tried to protect what it is they study by wrapping it in a stainless steel essence that cannot be criticized or gainsaid by those who are perceived to want to do it harm.

Esposito's goal in *Unholy War* is to show that there is not a "clash of civilizations" between the West and the Muslim world, and that Islam, "like Judaism and Christianity, rejects terrorism" (2003, xi). Implicit in the title of his book, Esposito implies that violence or terror when committed in the name of Islam (or any other religion) cannot be a religious act; that it must be an inauthentic or misplaced expression of religious zeal. For instance, he writes:

> The terrorists responsible for the atrocities of September 11, 2001, are the radical fringe of a broad-based Islamic jihad that began in the late twentieth century. Islam's power and the idealistic concepts of jihad have been "spun" to become the primary idiom of Muslim politics, used by rulers and ruled, by reformers, political opposition, and terrorists (2003, 73).

Here Esposito tries to show that the grievances felt by the likes of Osama bin Laden are by no means representative of a monolithic Islam, but represent a "radical fringe" that appeals to a set of Islamic symbols (e.g., jihad) and sentiments (e.g., *ressentiment*) that function to legitimate their project. Despite the attempts at nuance, Esposito still fails to acknowledge that lexemes such as jihad are potentially much more dynamic than he makes them out to be. Such terms do not possess fixed meanings or linguistic reifications that remain unchanged through an equally fixed Islamic history. On the contrary, such terms are the sites of semantic skirmishes that are fought between rival groups claiming authenticity through self-legitimation.

Despite Esposito's desire to nuance Islam, to show that it is not monolithic and that it admits of variety, he nonetheless resorts, as in his earlier writings, to defending an apolitical essence that resides at the heart of something called "Islam." He concludes his book, for example, with the claim that

> there can be no excuse for terrorism in the name of Islam. Suicide attacks, bombings, assassinations in the name of any cause, whether justified in the name of God, justice or state security, are still terrorism (2003, 160).

Here Esposito seems to conflate events such as 9/11, the American-led coalition against Afghanistan and Iraq, and the Israeli government's selected assassination of Islamic militants.[3] Anyone, Esposito implies, who kills in the name of some higher cause – be it God, the state, or security – is culpable of the same crime. Instead, he seems to want to claim that future harmony resides in recognizing our common heritage and, presumably because of this "our common future":

> Never before have soft phrases like "building bridges of understanding" been more critical in a war that ultimately cannot be won simply by military power. Understanding and action go hand in hand for Muslims and non-Muslims alike. All of us are challenged to move beyond stereotypes, historic grievances, and religious differences, to recognize our shared values as well as interests, and to move collectively to build our common future (2003, xi).

So much for critical scholarship.

Reclaiming Islam: Putting Theory into Practice

An entirely different project, albeit one motivated by similar forces, has seen a group of Muslims try to reclaim their tradition by emphasizing its "progressive" elements. In a book reflecting these views, *Progressive Muslims*, its editor, Omid Safi, defines a "progressive Muslim" as

> one who is committed to the strangely controversial idea that the worth of a human being is measured by a person's character, not the oil under their soil, and not their flag. A progressive Muslim agenda is concerned with the ramifications of the premise that all members of humanity have this same intrinsic worth because, as the Qur'ān reminds us, each of us has the breath of God breathed into our being (2003, 3).

On a theological level, one could, I think, quite easily make the case that this is a noble initiative. What we have is a group of Muslims who are fed up with the fundamentalist version of Islam that downplays issues that are reflected in the book's subtitle: justice, gender, and pluralism. Although Safi and others in the volume do not overtly use the term "hijacking" to explain the takeover of an essential and peaceful Islam by groups that are more interested in political and ideological power, such an argument is nonetheless implicit. Safi writes:

> being a progressive Muslim is the determination to hold Muslim societies accountable for justice and pluralism. It means openly and purposefully resisting, challenging, and overthrowing structures of tyranny and injustice in these societies. At a general level, it means contesting injustices of gender apartheid (practiced by groups such as the Taliban), as well as the persecution of religious and ethnic minorities (undertaken by Saddam Hussein against the Kurds, etc.). It means exposing the violations of human rights and freedoms of speech, press, religion, and the right to dissent in Muslim countries such as Saudi Arabia, Turkey, Iran, Pakistan, Sudan, Egypt, and others. More specifically it means embracing and implementing a different vision of Islam that that offered by Wahhabi and neo-Wahhabi groups (2003, 2).

Implicit in all of these desiderata on the part of liberal or progressive Muslims is the assumption that there exists a liberal or progressive Islam that is somehow compatible with all of these critiques. Moreover, this essential Islam, deriving from the Qur'ān and rarely later Islamic sources, is compatible with modernity, liberal values, and so on. The flipside is that all those types of islams – e.g., those practiced by the Taliban, Saddam Hussein, Wahhabi and neo-Wahhabi groups – are somehow inauthentic precisely because they stray from this self-styled "straight path." All of these islams, however, are constructed in the images of those doing the constructing , mirroring their concerns, issues, and socio-economic positions. Even though they may be uncomfortable by the comparison, groups such as neo-Wahhabis and progressive Muslims are doing precisely the same thing: arguing that there exists an Islamic kernel somewhere in the ether or in a particular collection of texts and that it becomes the goal of each group to provide the epistemological, religious, and intellectual categories to usher in their particular brand of Islam.

Certainly on one level the contributors to such a project are to be commended. Qua Muslims they have a desire to change the world for the better based on what they consider to be the noblest teachings of their tradition. This is an admirable *theological* project. As such, *Progressive Muslims* should form the basis of theological discussion, and perhaps hopefully pave the way for inter-faith dialogue groups to talk to one another in a meaningful and productive way that carves out various commonalities between this type of Islam and equally constructed versions of liberal Judaisms and Christianities.[4] However, and this is the only reason

5 The Implosion of a Discipline

I mention the book in this setting, all of the contributors to this volume are professors of Islamic studies.

For example, many of the contributors to *Progressive Muslims* are intimately involved with the Study of Islam section at the American Academy of Religion, those responsible for drafting the response to the attacks of 9/11 mentioned above. At the AAR many of these scholars have presented a series of panel discussions meant to articulate this liberal Islamic vision. A description of a 2003 panel, for example, gives the following account of the group's goals and motivations:

> This panel aims to present and analyze the emergence of the movement known as Progressive Islam. There is today a nascent community of Muslim activists and intellectuals who readily identify with the term "progressive Muslims." Progressive refers to a relentless striving towards a universal notion of justice in which no single community's prosperity, righteousness, and dignity comes at the expense of another. This movement is also Islamic, since it involves openness to rethinking fundamental assumptions about Islamic thought and practice. Central to this notion of a progressive Muslim identity are themes such as social justice, gender justice, and pluralism. The panelists will not present formal papers, but rather will lead a conversation in which they will discuss the relevance of various issues for this emerging Progressive Islamic identity. The format will be a dynamic one, consisting of brief informative presentations by panelists, followed by audience questions, critique, and participation (http://www.aarweb.org/annualmeet/2003/pbook/abstract.asp?ANum=A93&KeyWord=&B1=Submit#results).

In a particular venue, i.e., a theological or inter-faith colloquium, such a topic might well be appropriate and/or even necessary. However, at a major religious studies conference, especially one whose mandate is at least in theory (but rarely in practice) the objective study of religion, such a topic, I would argue, is completely out of place. The goal of the academic study of Islam, as I have tried to make clear throughout this study, should be the ways in which various groups appeal to some constructed authentic past and sources in order to legitimate their particular regime of truth. The history of Islam, like the history of any religion, is essentially the skirmishes that revolve around these regimes. The goal of the academic study of Islam is not to present scholars using themselves as their primary data to construct an essential Islam that appeals to an ideally constructed past in order to legitimate their project. This is not scholarship; it is, nothing more or less, than advocacy. And, as I move towards the conclusion of this study, this type of apologetics passing for scholarship represents all that is wrong with the academic study of Islam at the current moment. Yet, given the various genealogies that this book has tried to trace, it is perhaps not all that surprising.

Conclusion: Towards a Future Imperfect

> It was the best of times, it was the worst of times,
> it was the age of wisdom, it was the age of foolishness,
> it was the epoch of belief, it was the epoch of incredulity,
> it was the season of Light, it was the season of Darkness,
> it was the spring of hope, it was the winter of despair,
> we had everything before us, we had nothing before us
> we were all going direct to Heaven, we were all going direct the other way –
> in short, the period was so far like the present period,
> that some of its noisiest authorities insisted on its
> being received, for good or evil, in the superlative degree of comparison only
> (Dickens 1958 [1859], 1).

Charles Dickens's opening of *A Tale of Two Cities* strikes me as an appropriate way to understand the current moment in which Islamic studies, and its practitioners, finds itself. A quick perusal of the "Openings" page on the American Academy of Religion's website since 9/11 witnesses a massive number of positions for specialists in Islamic data, something that is extremely disproportionate when compared with the need for specialists in other religions or areas. On one hand, this has created unprecedented possibilities and opportunities for students of Islam. Virtually overnight, the Western world has taken an interest in this field of study, is reading the work produced by Islamicists, and for the most part is genuinely concerned with what such specialists have to say about this religion. Islamicists at universities throughout North America are frequently called upon in the media to comment on or nuance things Islamic, or to try and correct popular misconceptions. Yet, as I argued in the previous chapter, the events of 9/11 and more recent events have caught many Islamicists off guard. Many, especially in the United States, have been put on the defensive, forced to articulate a normative Islam often with appeals to concepts that scholars in other disciplines regard as highly problematical.

This desire to appeal to the rhetoric of essences, as I suggested in previous chapters, can be used to establish normative judgments about which one of the many islams out there is to be granted the status of "authentic." Such appeals represent the single biggest dilemma currently facing the academic study of Islam: The use of categories like "religion," "experience," and "culture" that are often completely devoid of links to

Conclusion

the ways that such terms are interrogated in cognate disciplines (e.g., cultural studies, diaspora studies). Yet, framed positively, I would like to suggest how this rather sad state of affairs within Islamic studies, *if understood properly*, might well illumine the larger discipline of religious studies. Contrary to the tenor of the majority of this study, in the few pages that remain, I here try to show how the academic study of Islam *potentially* has much promise and might well function as a catalyst to help us examine some of the unstable concepts and traditional assumptions that are so often taken for granted in the academic study of religion.

One of the great potentialities that the academic study of Islam possesses is its ability to be at the forefront of our thinking about religion and the way this term is alternatively imagined, reimagined, constructed, and reconstructed not only by practitioners but also by the academy. Islam, as many have shown (e.g., Rodinson 1987; Hentsch 1992; Masuzawa 2005), has been constructed as the anti-West, an amorphous container into which have been placed all those values and characteristics that we find unsavory and that we define as not-Us. This should certainly not come as a surprise; yet perhaps the theoretical underpinnings of these constructions for the academic study of religion have yet to be fully appreciated. I have frequently discussed above the manifold ways in which Islamicists have adopted and adapted (and continue to do so) the *sui generis* discourses employed in religious studies, but the issues could just as easily be reformulated to ask: At what point did religionists gravitate to Islam? Why did they suddenly find this religion to be a valid object of study after years of studying Hinduism, Buddhism, Christianity, and Judaism? In other words, what prejudices does the adoption of Islam as part of the religious studies' curriculum of world religions reveal about the state of the academic study of religion, and the questions it deems significant or not?

Moreover, in terms of constructing something amorphous such as religion, the current struggles in the so-called Muslim world show us clearly the problematic nature of the very term religion and might well prove a valuable check to those in the field of religious studies who feel quite comfortable speaking of traditions in the singular. It is quite obvious in looking at the current geopolitical moment that Islam is anything but a unified or coherent entity; on the contrary, it means many different things to many different people, and many appeal to what they consider to be a normative Islam based on a host of ideological, political, economic, gendered, and social factors. Perhaps more than any other religion today, Islam demonstrates how practitioners actively improvise on a host of idioms that have been deemed, for a variety of reasons, transcendent.

The academic study of Islam also has much to show us when it comes to revealing our own presuppositions of what religion means or should mean. Rather than regard events such as 9/11 as having nothing whatsoever to do with religion, as many have tried to argue, we can actually increase our awareness and understanding of religious discourses by realizing that religion at its roots need not have anything whatsoever to do with morality. Although particular religious idioms might well do so, religion does not necessarily make the world a better place to live in, nor does it unambiguously orient people toward a triumvirate of the good, the beautiful, or the just. A large part of what we construct as religious often blurs many of the distinctions and boundaries that embed this phenomena in other social and cultural forms. When we remove religion from such forms, it ceases to be a force of world peace or social justice, but can just as easily be dangerous and destructive. Yet, the way we have constructed religion through various theories that are full of all sorts of assumptions has largely served as a protection against such truths (see the comments in Orsi 2005, 187–92).

I certainly have no intention of suggesting that Islam is any more prone to violence than any other cultural formation that has been sublimated by its manifold practitioners. However, because Islam is everywhere these days, it provides a convenient segue into contextualizing and understanding the messiness of religion on the ground. It seems to me, then, that the academic study of Islam has a lot to contribute to the new conceptual modeling that is currently going on in the academic study of religion. Unfortunately most religious studies departments are still stuck in the "one religion, one expert" model (with the exception of Christianity, which usually has five or six so-called experts).

Yet, as I have suggested time and again above, there has been a real resistance on the part of Islamicists to engage in this type of critical activity. I contend, however, that scholars of Islam must reach out to other disciplines – to religious studies, to cultural studies, to diaspora studies, to sociology, to history, to anthropology, to political science, etc. – in order to examine the study of Islam in as wide a web as possible. I would go so far as to argue that Islam can only be studied in such an interdisciplinary or multidisciplinary environment.

For example, an interest in cultural studies can reveal that too often both scholars of Islam and of religion fall into the trap of writing as though communities constitute themselves through a simple recuperation of a true essence (e.g., "Muslimness," "Jewishness," or "Christianness"), ignoring the task of communal reinvention, and the challenge of enforcing the bounds of community. Rarely do we try to explain identity (whether personal or collective) as something contingent, in constant need of maintenance, reinvention, and repair. By emphasizing these features of identity, we see emerge a new emphasis on boundaries, especially various points of contact and repulsion. A focus on boundaries leads us to the methodological urgency of questioning their given nature.

Moreover, a renewed interest in the literary and ideological component of the Qur'ān and early Islamic sources might begin to reveal important insights into the various ways that so-called new religions think with so-called older ones. What gets lost when a religion encounters other religions? How does an earlier message change? And, perhaps more importantly, why the change? What, in other words, are the ideological, political, and sociological factors and repercussions of various religions bumping up against one another? Here, I would argue that more work needs to be done on the types of questions asked by the likes of Abraham Geiger, who I discussed in Chapter 1. Obviously, however, and as I argued there, we cannot simply pick up Geiger's conceptual vocabulary and categories as if they were brand new. However, we can certainly entertain how earlier Judaic and Christian messages contributed to early Muslim self-understanding and socio-rhetorical formations.

Some of my own work (e.g., 2004a), for example, has examined the many diverse subcultures in medieval Islam, especially in al-Andalus, or Muslim Spain. Many of these subcultures (e.g., Jews, Christians, philosophers, Isma'ilis, Sufis) spoke a common discourse (both literal [i.e., Arabic], and metaphorical [i.e., in the categories they used to imagine and understand the world]). All of these groups made rival claims to the effect that they somehow had the keys to unlock the secrets of monotheism – and they all did so using the same conceptual vocabulary. As a result, they developed notions of authority, hermeneutics, and gnosis often in ways that were consciously juxtaposed with or subversive of the claims made by other subcultures. Methodologically, it is worth examining the points of contact, both literal and literary, between these subcultures, trying both to problematize and theorize about how groups think with other groups in the process of socio-rhetorical self-definition. This allows us not only a window onto the margins of the Islamic world, but also on the margins of those margins.

This study has attempted to chart a possible course for the future of Islamic studies as it thinks about its role, place, and modes of being in departments of religious studies. The only way to move forward, as I have constantly intimated here, is to be extremely self-reflexive and self-conscious of the critical discourses that have shaped how Islamicists construct and continue to construct theories meant to explain adequately their data. Here, however, it is necessary to be aware that data discovered do not simply exist naturally in the world waiting to be discovered, but that data emerge through questions asked (or not) of material deemed to be significant (or again not). This is why it is central that practitioners of

Islamic studies be aware of whence the discourses they employ derive. Only by examining the various ways in which Islamic studies identifies its discursive formations, establishes its critical practices, and links up with other disciplinary units or sub-units will we be able to glimpse, albeit ephemerally, at the various intellectual, social, cultural and rhetorical stuff of what it is we do or at least think it is that we do. Framed broadly, I have argued that central to our craft is the realization that the questions we formulate are as fundamentally in history and culture as the actors and texts that we purport to study. As a result, it is imperative that we understand how we got from there to here, that we are constantly vigilant lest we mistake the inherited for the axiomatic, and that we be aware that our theoretical paradigms are as influenced by economic, social, political, and ideological factors as they are by the discovery of newer or better data. Only by engaging in such interrogations will we be self-reflexive of how and why we have situated Islam as we have done, and as we will no doubt continue to do in the future.

Notes

Introduction

1. Because I am arguing for both the artificially constructed nature of academic disciplines and the need to dismantle the disciplinary fences that separate contiguous departments, I do not capitalize the names of disciplines in what follows.

Chapter 1

1   In the 1890s, the Cambridge Mission in Delhi approached Miss F. M. Young to translate the work into English. Their hope was that if Muslims realized the Jewish background of their sacred scripture they might convert to Christianity.
2   In the various political wars for who controls Middle Eastern studies in the American Academy, there has been a movement to discredit Said's claim to Jerusalem (see, e.g., Weiner 1999). Even if this were true, which I doubt it is, it would have no impact on either Said's argument or its influence.
3   Parts of this section and the following one draw upon and develop published material in Hughes 2005, 2006.
4   The fact that Jesus was a Jew caused many of these historians a great deal of problems. Some even went so far as to suggest that Jesus' racial identity was probably Aryan and that his real goal was the destruction of Judaism. Such views, not surprisingly, became increasingly popular, culminating in the mythology of the Third Reich (Heschel 1998, 11–12).
5   Here it is important to remember that what we today recognize as various "branches" of Judaism – e.g., Reform, Conservative, Orthodox – did not yet exist. Although there was a tendency for certain Jewish thinkers to propose liberal policy, something that would eventually crystallize as "Reform Judaism," this had not yet occurred. Indeed, Geiger would be an important catalyst in this process.
6   A more nuanced account may be found in Hentsch, who argues that the historical relations between the Orient and the Occident have been much more complicated than Said would lead us to believe (1992, xii–xiv, 23–48).
7   This is not to say that such work is not valuable or even desired. My only point here is that it is an approach that downplays historical contexts and, instead, emphasizes phenomenological ones. Examples of such important works include Graham 1977; Sells 1999.
8   This is the way that Newby (1988, 105) in his otherwise excellent study of the Jews of Arabia characterizes Geiger's methodology. In fact, as I have tried to argue here, Geiger's scholarship represents an important tempering when compared to others.

Chapter 2

1   It is equally important to call attention to the fact that notice of Islam and the Islamic world during the formative period of Middle Eastern studies in the United States showed virtually no interest in Islam or the Islamic world existing outside of the Middle East, where the overwhelming majority of Muslims live. Only during the last decade or so has this begun to shift.

2   It is important to realize, however, that area studies did not simply grow out of the cold war; indeed, as some have argued, their growth might actually have been impeded by wartime activity (e.g., Szanton 2004, 3–4).

3   This perceived double standard is part of Kramer's highly cynical overview of the state of the field of Middle Eastern Studies in the US (e.g., 2001, 91–99), to be discussed in greater detail in Chapter 5 below. Moreover, since 9/11, many Americans and American legislators have called into question the funding of Middle Eastern studies primarily because they are highly critical of what they perceive to be overly liberal academics who are critical of American policy initiatives.

4   My use of the figures that appear in Kramer 2001 should in no way be taken as a personal endorsement, tacit or otherwise, of Kramer's main thesis that the apologetical enterprise inherent in Middle Eastern and/or Islamic studies failed to predict the 9/11 attacks.

5   The department is now called the "Gustav E. Grunebaum Center for Near Eastern Studies."

6   Of the eight books in the series of which *Unity and Variety in Muslim Civilization* was a part, three were devoted to Islam, two to China, and one to India.

7   Just in case we are uncertain of Lewis's touchstone, he reminds us: 'I believe that parliamentary democracy as practiced in the West, with all its manifest faults, is still the best and most just form of government yet devised by man. But at the same time I believe it to be the most difficult to operate, requiring certain qualities of mind and habit, of institution and tradition, perhaps even of climate, for its effective working. It has taken firm root only among the peoples of the northern and north-western fringes of Europe, and in the territories colonized by their descendents overseas' (1954, 2).

8   Nowhere is this more prevalent than in the writings of Mircea Eliade (1907–1986), whose twin notions of religion as *sui generis* and the unique ability of the history of religions to uncover this aspect of religion is notorious (see critiques in, e.g., Strenski 1982, 1987; McCutcheon 1997, 74–100) yet still popular.

Chapter 3

1   It is probably no coincidence that Cantwell Smith's essay (1959) appears in the volume on methodology edited by Eliade and Kitagawa. In this volume, like those that would come after it, we find a useful introduction to the preoccupations of most (if not all) of the writers represented in all three volumes: the call for taking religion

'seriously' (which generally functions as a codeword for the non-reductive discourse on *sui generis* religion); speculations, based upon no theoretical argumentation concerning just what counts as a religion, in the enduring presence of the 'basically religious'; the contemporary social utility of the findings of this discipline; the need to use historical investigation in the service of accessing deeper, ahistorical universals" (McCutcheon 2003, 65).

2   As Bryan Turner has argued, Hodgson's take on religious piety, especially the tension between piety/individual and religion/society, is shaped by his Quaker background (Turner 1994, 60–66). This leads Turner to conclude that

> In *The Venture of Islam*, we are presented with a history of Islamicate societies determined by the inner history of personal piety. The institutionalized shell of law, economics, political organization is thereby secondary to the sociologically unfettered dynamics of man's inner response to God. Because Hodgson wants to protect piety in this way and because he wants to treat the main articulation of piety as art, poetry, and philosophy, Hodgson is in fact forced into the arms of philology and Orientalism from which he wants to extricate the study of Islam (1994, 66).

3   Not coincidentally, Rahman 1982 is a work devoted to responding to errors he perceives to be made by various Islamists who try to construct a normative Islam made in their own image. Of course, Rahman himself does something similar, only his construction is much more "safe" and in keeping with values deemed "liberal." Perhaps for this reason this work was well funded, as the preface makes clear, by "a generous grant from the Ford foundation."

4   Not coincidentally, Moosa was responsible for editing and introducing Rahman 2000.

Chapter 4

1   Here I note, but do not explore, the tremendous gap between the ways in which "identity" is interrogated in cultural studies and the rather lame assumptions that inform such concepts in religious studies. The latter must, and I will address this briefly in the conclusion to this study, take into consideration the findings of the former.

2   McCutcheon also notes that this volume succeeded in establishing a genealogy for the "Chicago School" of religion by ignoring European scholars of religion and giving pride of place to students and faculty of the Divinity School (2003, 69–70).

3   I have responded to Adams's claims in other contexts for different purposes (see, in particular, Hughes 2003, 2004b).

4   Jerry Falwell, for example, is on record as saying: "I think Mohammed was a terrorist. I read enough of the history of his life, written by both Muslims and non-Muslims, that he was a violent man, a man of war… In my opinion…I do believe that – Jesus set the example for love, as did Moses. And I think that Mohammed set an opposite example" (http://www.cbsnews.com/stories/2002/10/03/60minutes/main524268.shtml).

5   One of the few introductory books to take such questions seriously is Rippin (2001a). He writes that "How did the Qur'an come to look the way it does, with the subject matter within individual chapters jumping from one topic to the next, with duplications and inconsistencies in grammar, law and theology abounding? To the source critic, the work displays all the tendencies of rushed editing with only the most superficial concern for the content, the editors/compilers apparently engaged only in establishing a fixed text of scripture" (23; in this regard also see Cook 1996 [1983], 73–76).

6   This passage is also quoted in McCutcheon (2005, 62–63), whose discussion I endorse and draw upon.

7   Although in 2006, Armstrong gave one of the main plenary addresses at the annual meeting of the American Academy of Religion (AAR), the major venue of and for professional religionists in North America.

8   Here it might well be worth pointing out just how omnipresent this liberal Protestant discourse is when a former nun buys into it without even questioning its credentials.

Chapter 5

1   I would like to thank my friend Elliot R. Wolfson for bringing the lyrics of this Dylan song to my attention.

2   I think it worth noting that the main discussion list for Islamicists in religious studies (the Islamaar listserve) circulated, or let circulate, the now infamous and ridiculous message stating that it was Israel's Mossad that was responsible for the attacks and that Jews were told to "stay home" on the day in question.

3   Martin Kramer is extremely critical of Esposito's position on this. Although writing before the publication of *Unholy War*, Kramer says the following about Esposito:

> Esposito came forward to claim that Islamist movements were nothing other than movements of democratic reform. Only Orientalist prejudice, of the kind dissected by Said, prevented American observers from seeing past external form to this inner quality (2001, 50).

4   For example, in a footnote Safi writes: "I am here reminded of the similarity of this Islamic perspective to the Jewish mystical concept of *Tikkun olam*, which calls humanity to be responsible for healing the world through concrete acts of righteousness and goodness, alongside mystical meditations on the Divine spheres. May this be one bridge we can use to bring like-minded and like-hearted Muslims and Jews together to heal our communities, as we seek to heal this world" (2003, 29 n. 31). As someone interested in Jews and Muslims talking to one another, I could not agree more. However, it is necessary to be clear in what capacity participants in such conversations should speak. Does one do this as a professor of religious studies or as a Jew/Muslim? Safi, and the overwhelming majority of the contributors in this volume, is never particularly clear on this blurring of capacities. The result is ambiguous. In what capacity are they speaking? To whom? For whom?

Bibliography

Adams, Charles J. 1967. "The History of Religions and the Study of Islam." In Joseph M. Kitagawa, Mircea Eliade, and Charles H. Long, eds, *The History of Religions: Essays on the Problem of Understanding*, 177–93. Chicago: University of Chicago Press.
Ahmad, Aijaz. 1992. "*Orientalism* and After: Ambivalence and Metropolitan Location in the Work of Edward Said." In idem, *In Theory: Classes, Nations, Literatures*, 159–219. New York: Verso.
Anidjar, Gil. 2003. *The Jew, The Arab: A History of the Enemy*. Stanford: Stanford University Press.
Armstrong, Karen. 2000. *Islam: A Short History*. New York: The Modern Library.
_____. 2001. "The True, Peaceful Face of Islam." *Time* (October 1): 48.
Arnal, William E. 2005. *The Symbolic Jesus: Historical Scholarship, Judaism and the Construction of Contemporary Identity*. London: Equinox.
Asad, Talal, ed. 1973. *Anthropology and the Cultural Encounter*. Amherst, NY: Humanity Books.
Ayoub, Mahmoud M. 2002. "The Islamic Tradition." In Willard G. Oxtoby, ed., *World Religions: Western Traditions*, 341–461. 2nd ed. New York: Oxford University Press.
Berg, Herbert. 2000. *The Development of Exegesis in Early Islam: The Authenticity of Muslim Literature from the Formative Period*. Richmond, Surrey: Curzon.
_____, ed. 2003. *Method and Theory in the Study of Islamic Origins*. Leiden: Brill.
Binder, Leonard, 1976. "Area Studies: A Critical Reassessment." In idem, *The Study of the Middle East: Research and Scholarship in the Humanities and Social Sciences*, 1–28. New York: John Wiley and Sons.
Brauer, Jerald C. 1967. "General Editor's Preface." In Joseph M. Kitagawa, Mircea Eliade, and Charles H. Long, eds, *The History of Religions: Essays on the Problem of Understanding*, v–x. Chicago: University of Chicago Press.
Cantwell Smith, Wilfred. See under Smith, Wilfred Cantwell.
Cohen, Mark R. 1994. *Under Crescent and Cross: The Jews in the Middle Ages*. Princeton: Princeton University Press.
Conrad, Lawrence I. 1999. "Ignaz Goldziher on Ernst Renan: From Orientalist Philology to the Study of Islam." In Martin Kramer, ed., *The Jewish Discovery of Islam: Studies in Honor of Bernard Lewis*, 137–80. Tel Aviv: Tel Aviv University Press.
Cook, Michael. 1996 [1983]. *Muhammad*. Oxford: Oxford University Press.
Cracknell, Kenneth, ed. 2001. *Wilfred Cantwell Smith: A Reader*. Oxford: Oneworld.
Crone, Patricia. 1987. *Meccan Trade and the Rise of Islam*. Princeton: Princeton University Press.
Crone, Patricia, and Michael Cook. 1977. *Hagarism: The Making of the Islamic World*. Cambridge: Cambridge University Press.
Daniel, Norman. 1997. *Islam and the West: The Making of an Image*. Oxford: Oneworld.
Denny, Frederick Mathewson. 1994. *An Introduction to Islam*. 2nd ed. New York: Macmillan.

———. 2006. *An Introduction to Islam*. 3rd ed. New York: Macmillan.
Dickens, Charles. 1958 [1859]. *A Tale of Two Cities*. London: J.M. Dent and Sons.
Dubuisson, Daniel. 2003. *The Western Construction of Religion: Myths, Knowledge, and Ideology*. Trans. William Sayers. Baltimore: Johns Hopkins University Press.
Duchesne-Guillemin, Jacques. 1955. "How Does Islam Stand?" In Gustav E. von Grunebaum, ed., *Unity and Variety in Muslim Civilization*, 3–14. Chicago: University of Chicago Press.
Durkheim, Emile and Marcel Mauss. 1969 [1903]. *Primitive Classification*. Trans. Rodney Needlam. Chicago: University of Chicago Press.
Eagleton, Terry. 1991. *Ideology: An Introduction*. New York: Verso.
Eliade, Mircea. 1958. *Patterns in Comparative Religion*. Trans. Rosemary Sheed. New York: Sheed and Ward.
———. 1959. *The Sacred and the Profane: The Nature of Religion*. Trans. Willard R. Trask. San Diego: Harvest/HBJ.
Esposito, John L. 1999 [1992]. *The Islamic Threat: Myth or Reality?* 3rd ed. New York: Oxford University Press.
———. 2003. *Unholy War: Terror in the Name of Islam*. New York: Oxford University Press.
———. 2005 [1988]. *Islam: The Straight Path*. Rev. 3rd edn. New York: Oxford University Press.
Ferahian, Salwa. 2001. "W.C. Smith Remembered." *MELA Notes* 64. http://www.lib.umich.edu/area/Near.East/toc64.html
Firestone, Reuven. 1990. *Journeys in Holy Lands: The Evolution of the Abraham-Ishmael Legends in Islamic Exegesis*. Albany: State University of New York Press.
Fitzgerald, Timothy. 2000. *The Ideology of Religious Studies*. New York: Oxford University Press.
Fleischer, H. L. 1841. "Über das Arabische in Dr. Geigers Preisschrift: *Was hat Muhammad aus den Judenthume aufgenommen?*" *Der Orient: Literaturblatt des Orients*; reprinted in Fleischer, *Kleinere Schriften* 2 (1888): 107–38.
Fück, Johann, 1955. *Die Arabischen Studien in Europa bis in den Anfang des 20 Jahrhunderts*. Leipzig: O. Harassowitz.
Geertz, Clifford. 2003. "Which Way to Mecca?" *The New York Review of Books* 50 (July 3): 36–39.
Geiger, Abraham. 1835. *Was hat Mohammed aus dem Judenthume aufgenommen?* Bonn: F. Baaden.
———. 1836. "Die Gründung einer jüdisch-theologischen Facultät, ein dringendes Bedürfniß unserer Zeit." *Wissenschaftliche Zeitschrift für jüdische Theologie* 2: 6.
———. 1970 [1835]. *Judaism and Islam*. Trans. F. M. Young. Madras: MDCSPK Press; repr. New York: Ktav, 1970.
———. 1985 [1865]. *Judaism and Its History*. Lanham, MD: University Press of America.
———. 2005. *Was hat Mohammed aus dem Judenthume aufgenommen?* Berlin: Parega.
Geiger, Ludwig. 1910. *Abraham Geiger: Leben und Lebenswerk*. Berlin: G. Reimer.
Gibb, H. A. R. 1972 [1947]. *Modern Trends in Islam*. Chicago: University of Chicago Press; repr. New York: Octagon Books.
Gold, Daniel. 2003. *Aesthetics and Analysis in Writing on Religion: Modern Fascinations*. Berkeley: University of California Press.

Bibliography

Graham, William. 1977. *Divine Word and Prophetic Word in Early Islam: A Reconsideration of the Sources with Special Reference to the Divine Sayings or Hadith Qudsi*. The Hague: Mouton.

von Grunebaum, Gustav E. 1955. "The Problem: Unity in Diversity." In idem, *Unity and Variety in Muslim Civilization*, 17–37. Chicago: University of Chicago Press.

Hall, Robert B. 1947. *Area Studies: With Special Reference to Their Implications for Research in the Social Sciences*. New York: Social Science Research Council.

Hegel, G. W. F. 1953 [1837]. *Reason in History: A General Introduction to the Philosophy of History*. Trans. Robert S. Hartman. New York: Liberal Arts Press.

Hentsch, Thierry. 1992. *Imagining the Middle East*. Trans. Fred A. Reed. Montreal: Black Rose Books.

Heschel, Susannah. 1998. *Abraham Geiger and the Jewish Jesus*. Chicago: University of Chicago Press.

Hirschfeld, Hartwig. 1878. *Jüdische Elemente in Koran*. Berlin: n.p.

Hobsbawm, Eric J., ed. 1992. *The Invention of Tradition*. Cambridge: Cambridge University Press.

Hodgson, Marshall G. S. 1974. *The Venture of Islam: Conscience and History in a World Civilization*. I: *The Classical Age of Islam*. Chicago: University of Chicago Press.

Horovitz, Joseph. 1925. "Jewish Proper Names and Derivatives in the Koran." *Hebrew Union College Annual* 2: 145–227.

———. 2002 [1927]. *The Earliest Biographies of the Prophet and their Authors*. Ed. Lawrence I. Conrad. Princeton: Darwin Press.

Hughes, Aaron W. 2003. "The Stranger at the Sea: Mythopoesis in the Qur'ān and Early Tafsīr." *Studies in Religion* 32.3: 261–79.

———. 2004a. *The Texture of the Divine: Imagination in Medieval Islamic and Jewish Thought*. Bloomington: Indiana University Press.

———. 2004b. "Mapping Constructions of Islamic Space in North America: A Framework for Further Inquiry." *Studies in Religion* 33.3-4: 339–57.

———. 2005. "The 'Golden Age' of Muslim Spain: Religious Identity and the Invention of a Tradition in Modern Jewish Studies." In Steven Engler and Gregory P. Grieve, eds, *Historicizing Tradition in the Study of Religion*, 51–74. Berlin: de Gruyter.

———. 2006. "Outside Looking In: An Epilogue (of Sorts)." *Studies in Religion* 35.3–4: 561–75.

Institute of Islamic Studies, McGill University. 2006. "Requirements for the Ph.D. Programme." Available as pdf file at: http://www.mcgill.ca/islamicstudies/programmes

James, William. 1990 [1902]. *The Varieties of Religious Experience*. New York: Vintage Books.

Juschka, Darlene M. 2006. "Interdisciplinarity in Religious and Women's Studies." *Studies in Religion* 35.3–4: 391–401.

Kippenberg, Hans G. 2002. *Discovering Religious History in the Modern Age*. Trans. Barbara Harshav. Princeton: Princeton University Press.

Koltun-Fromm, Ken. 2006. *Abraham Geiger's Liberal Judaism: Personal Meaning and Religious Authority*. Bloomington: Indiana University Press.

Kramer, Martin. 1999. "Introduction." In idem, ed., *The Jewish Discovery of Islam: Studies in Honor of Bernard Lewis*, 1–48. Tel Aviv: Tel Aviv University Press.

———. 2001. *Ivory Towers on Sand: The Failure of Middle Eastern Studies in America*. Washington: Washington Institute for Near East Policy.

Kugel, James L. 1990. *In Potiphar's House: The Interpretive Life of Biblical Texts*. San Francisco: Harper.

Kurtz, Stanley. 2003. "Reforming the Campus: Congress Targets Title VI." *National Review Online*. October 14. http://www.nationalreview.com/kurtz kurtz200310140905.asp

Laroui, Abdallah. 1976. *The Crisis of the Arab Intellectual: Traditionalism and Historicism*. Trans. Diarmid Cammell. Berkeley: University of California Press.

Lassner, Jacob. 1993. *Demonizing the Queen of Sheba*. Chicago: University of Chicago Press.

———. 1999. "Abraham Geiger: A Nineteenth-Century Jewish Reformer on the Origins of Islam." In Martin Kramer, ed., *The Jewish Discovery of Islam: Studies in Honor of Bernard Lewis*, 103–35. Tel Aviv: Tel Aviv University Press.

Levine, Mark. 2005. *Why They Don't Hate Us: Lifting the Veil on the Axis of Evil*. Oxford: Oneworld.

Lewis, Bernard. 1954. "Communism and Islam." *International Affairs* 3.1: 1–12.

———. 1955. "Turkey: Westernization." In Gustav E. von Grunebaum, ed., *Unity and Variety in Muslim Civilization*, 311–31. Chicago: University of Chicago Press.

———. 1982a. "The Question of Orientalism." *New York Review of Books* (June 24): 49–56.

———. 1982b. "Reply to Edward Said." *New York Review of Books* (August 12): 46–48.

———. 1993. "The Pro-Islamic Jews." In idem, *Islam in History: Ideas, Peoples, and Events in the Middle East*, rev. ed., 137–52. Chicago: Open Court.

———. 2003. *What Went Wrong? The Clash Between Islam and Modernity in the Middle East*. New York: Perennial.

Lincoln, Bruce. 1989. *Discourse and the Construction of Society: Comparative Studies of Myth, Ritual, and Classification*. New York: Oxford University Press.

———. 1994. *Authority: Construction and Corrosion*. Chicago: University of Chicago Press.

———. 1996. "Theses on Method." *Method & Theory in the Study of Religion* 8.3: 225–27.

———. 1999. *Theorizing Myth: Narrative, Ideology, and Scholarship*. Chicago: University of Chicago Press.

———. 2003. *Holy Terrors: Thinking About Religion After September 11*. Chicago: University of Chicago Press.

Lockman, Zachary. 2004a. *Contending Visions of the Middle East: The History and Politics of Orientalism*. Cambridge: Cambridge University Press.

———. 2004b. "Behind the Battles over US Middle East Studies." *Interventions: Middle East Report Online*. January. http://www.merip.org/mero/interventions/lockman_interv.html

Lopez Jr., Donald S. 1998. *Prisoners of Shangri-La: Tibetan Buddhism and the West*. Chicago: University of Chicago Press.

Mack, Michael. 2003. *German Idealism and the Jew: The Inner Anti-Semitism of Philosophy and German-Jewish Responses*. Chicago: University of Chicago Press.

Bibliography

Martin, Richard C. 1998. "Fazlur Rahman's Contribution to Religious Studies: A Historian of Religion's Appraisal." In Earle H. Waugh and Fredrick M. Denny, eds, *The Shaping of an American Islamic Discourse: A Memorial to Fazlur Rahman*, 241–59. Atlanta: Scholars Press.

Masuzawa, Tomoko. 2005. *The Invention of World Religions: Or, How Universalism Was Preserved in the Language of Pluralism*. Chicago: University of Chicago Press.

McCutcheon, Russell T. 1997. *Manufacturing Religion: The Discourse on Sui Generis Religion and the Politics of Nostalgia*. New York: Oxford University Press.

———. 2003. *The Discipline of Religion: Structure, Meaning, and Rhetoric*. New York and London: Routledge.

———. 2005. *Religion and the Domestication of Dissent: Or, How to Live in a Less than Perfect Nation*. London: Equinox.

Mendes-Flohr, Paul. 1991. "Fin de Siècle Orientalism, the *Ostjuden*, and the Aesthetics of Jewish Self-Affirmation." In idem, *Divided Passions: Jewish Intellectuals and the Experience of Modernity*, 77–132. Detroit: Wayne State University Press.

Moosa, Ebrahim. 2005. *Ghazālī and the Poetics of Imagination*. Chapel Hill: University of North Carolina Press.

Myers, David N. 1995. *Re-Inventing the Jewish Past: European Jewish Intellectuals and the Zionist Return to History*. New York: Oxford University Press.

———. 1997. "The Ideology of Wissenschaft des Judentums." In Daniel H. Frank and Oliver Leaman, eds, *The History of Jewish Philosophy*, 706–20. London: Routledge.

Nandy, Ashis. 1992. *The Intimate Enemy: Loss and Recovery of Self Under Colonialism*. Delhi: Oxford University Press.

Nanji, Azim, ed. 1997. *Mapping Islamic Studies: Genealogy, Continuity and Change*. New York and Berlin: Mouton de Gruyter.

Nasr, Seyyed Hossein. 2002. *The Heart of Islam: Enduring Values for Humanity*. San Francisco: HarperSanFrancisco.

Newby, Gordon D. 1988. *A History of the Jews of Arabia: From Ancient Times to Their Eclipse Under Islam*. Columbus: University of South Carolina Press.

Nietzsche, Friedrich Wilhelm. 1954 [1873]. "On Truth and Lie in an Extra-Moral Sense." In Walter Kaufmann, ed. and trans., *The Portable Nietzsche*, 42–47. Harmondsworth: Penguin.

Nöldeke, Theodor. 1938. *Geschichte des Qorans*. Ed. Friedrich Schwally. 2nd ed. Leipzig: T. Dieter.

Novick, Peter. 1988. *That Noble Dream: The "Objectivity Question" and the American Historical Profession*. Cambridge: Cambridge University Press.

Orsi, Robert A. 2005. *Between Heaven and Earth: The Religious Worlds People Make and the Scholars Who Study Them*. Princeton: Princeton University Press.

Owen, Roger. 1973. "Studying Islamic History." *Journal of Interdisciplinary History* 4.2: 287–98.

Pearlman, Moshe. 1970. "Prolegomenon." In Abraham Geiger, *Judaism and Islam*, vii–xxvi. Trans. F.M. Young. New York: Ktav.

Preus, J. Samuel. 1987. *Explaining Religion: Criticism and Theory from Bodin to Freud*. New Haven: Yale University Press.

Proudfoot, Wayne. 1985. *Religious Experience*. Berkeley: University of California Press.

Putnam, Hilary, et al. 2001. "Wilfred Cantwell Smith: In Memoriam." *Harvard Gazette Archives* (November 29). http://www.hno.harvard.edu/gazette/2001/11.29/27-memorialminute.html

Rahman, Fazlur. 1979 [1966]. *Islam*. 2nd ed. Chicago: University of Chicago Press.

———. 1980. *Major Themes of the Qur'ān*. Minneapolis: Bibliotheca Islamica.

———. 1981 [1952]. *Avicenna's Psychology: An English Translation of Kitāb al-Najāt, Book II, chapter VI*. New York: Oxford University Press.

———. 1982. *Islam and Modernity: Transformation of an Intellectual Tradition*. Chicago: University of Chicago Press.

———. 2000. *Revival and Reform in Islam: A Study of Islamic Fundamentalism*. Edited and with an introduction by Ebrahim Moosa. Oxford: Oneworld.

von Ranke, Leopold. 1973 [1824–1880]. *The Theory and Practice of History*. Ed. and trans. George Iggers and Konrad von Moltke. Indianapolis: Bobbs-Merrill.

Rippin, Andrew. 2001a. *Muslims: Their Religious Beliefs and Practices*. 2nd ed. London and New York: Routledge.

———. 2001b. *The Qur'ān and Its Interpretive Tradition*. Aldershot, Hampshire and Burlington, Vermont: Ashgate/Variorum.

Rodinson, Maxime. 1987. *Europe and the Mystique of Islam*. Trans. Roger Venius. Seattle: University of Washington Press.

Safi, Omid, ed. 2003. *Progressive Muslims: On Justice, Gender, and Pluralism*. Oxford: Oneworld.

Said, Edward W. 1978. *Orientalism*. New York: Vintage.

———. 1980. *The Arab Image in Western Mass Media*. London: Outline Books.

———. 1982. "Orientalism: An Exchange." *New York Review of Books* (August 12): 44–46.

———. 1993. *Culture and Imperialism*. New York: Alfred A. Knopf.

Schaeder, Hans Heinrich. 1940. "Deutsche Orientforschung." *Der Nahe Osten* (Berlin) 1: 129–34.

Schapiro, Israel. 1907. *Die haggadischen Elemente im erzählended Teil des Korans*. Leipzig: Fock.

Scharf, Robert. 1999. "Experience." In Mark C. Taylor, ed., *Critical Terms for Religious Studies*, 70–93. Chicago: University of Chicago Press.

Schelling, F. W. J. 1966 [1803]. *On University Studies*. Trans. E. S. Morgan. Athens, OH: Ohio University Press.

Schorsch, Ismar. 1975. "Editor's Introduction: Ideology and History." In Heinrich Graetz, *The Structure of Jewish History and Other Essays*, 1–62. New York: Jewish Theological Seminary of America Press.

———. 1994. "Scholarship in the Service of Reform." In idem, *From Text to Context: The Return to History in Modern Judaism*, 303–33. Hanover: University Press of New England.

Sells, Michael. 1999. *Approaching the Qur'an: The Early Revelations*. Ashland, OR: White Cloud Press.

Shaw, Rosalind. 1995. "Feminist Anthropology and the Gendering of Religious Studies." In Ursula King, ed., *Religion and Gender*, 65–76. Oxford: Blackwell.

Smith, Jonathan Z. 1982. *Imagining Religion: From Babylon to Jonestown*. Chicago: University of Chicago Press.

Smith, Wilfred Cantwell. 1959. "Comparative Religion: Whither – and Why?" In Mircea Eliade and Joseph Kitagawa, eds, *The History of Religions: Essays in Methodology*, 31–58. Chicago: Univeristy of Chicago Press.
_____. 1962. *The Faith of Other Men*. San Francisco: Harper Torchbooks.
_____. 1981. *On Understanding Islam: Selected Studies*. The Hague: Mouton.
_____. 1991 [1962]. *The Meaning and End of Religion*. Foreword by John Hick. Minneapolis: Fortress.
Smock, David R. 1976. "Ford Foundation Support for Middle Eastern Studies in the U.S." *MESA Bulletin* 10.1: 20–25.
Speyer, Heinrich. 1931. *Biblischen Erzählungen im Qoran*. Berlin, 1931; repr. Hildesheim: Georg Olm Verlagsbuchhandlung, 1961.
Stetkevych, Jaroslav. 1996. *Muhammad and the Golden Bough: Reconstructing Arabian Myth*. Bloomington: Indiana University Press.
Steward, Julian H. 1950. *Area Research: Theory and Practice*. New York: Social Science Research Council.
Strenski, Ivan. 1982. "Love and Anarchy in Romania." Review of Mircea Eliade, *Autobiography*. *Religion* 12: 391–403.
_____. 1987. *Four Theories of Myth in Twentieth Century History*. Iowa City: University of Iowa Press.
Szanton, David L. 2004. "The Origin, Nature, and Challenges of Area Studies in the United States." In idem, *The Politics of Knowledge: Area Studies and the Disciplines*, 1–33. Berkeley: University of California Press.
Turner, Bryan S. 1994. *Orientalism, Postmodernism, and Globalization*. London and New York: Routledge.
Wallerstein, Immanuel. 1997. "The Unintended Consequences of Cold War Area Studies." In Noam Chomsky, ed., *The Cold War and the University: Toward an Intellectual History of the Postwar Years*, 195–231. New York: The New Press.
Wansbrough, John. 1977. *Quranic Studies: Sources and Methods of Scriptural Interpretation*. Oxford: Oxford University Press.
_____. 2001. *The Qurʾān: Style and Contents*. Ed. Andrew Rippin. Aldershot: Ashgate.
Wasserstrom, Steven M. 1999. *Religion After Religion: Gershom Scholem, Mircea Eliade, and Henry Corbin at Eranos*. Princeton: Princeton University Press.
Waugh, Earle H., and Frederick M. Denny, eds. 1998. *The Shaping of an American Islamic Discourse: A Memorial to Fazlur Rahman*. Atlanta: Scholars Press.
Weiner, Justus Reid. 1999. "'My Beautiful Old House' and Other Fabrications by Edward Said." *Commentary* 2 (September): 23–31.
White, Hayden. 1978. *Tropics of Discourse: Essays in Cultural Criticism*. Baltimore: Johns Hopkins University Press.
Wiebe, Donald. 1984. "The Failure of Nerve in the Academic Study of Religion." *Studies in Religion* 13.4: 401–22.
_____. 2006. "The Learned Practice of Religion: A Review of the History of Religious Studies in Canada and its Portent for the Future." *Studies in Religion* 35.3–4: 475–501.
Wiener, Max. 1981. *Abraham Geiger and Liberal Judaism: The Challenge of the Nineteenth Century*. Trans. Ernst J. Schlochauer. Cincinnati: Hebrew Union College Press.

Subject Index

A
Afghanistan 109
al-Qaeda 55, 85, 92, 101
American Academy of Religion (AAR) 98, 111–12, 120
anti-Semitism 11
apologetics 82–92
area studies 37–40, 42, 51–56, 102, 118
Army Specialized Training Program (ASTP) 37
authenticity 50–53, 83–84, 93
    rhetoric of 54–55, 61–62, 107
    see also Islam, "authentic" representations of

B
belief 50, 61–62, 81, 85–87, 99

C
Campus Watch 103–5
Carnegie Foundation 41
Central Intelligence Agency (CIA) 40, 42
Centre for the Study of World Religions (Harvard) 59, 64
Civil Affairs Training Schools (CATS) 37
classification 35–37, 52, 98
Cold War and Communism 35, 37, 51, 99
colonialism 11, 25–28, 34, 37, 44–45, 50–52 see also Orientalism
Commentary 103
congressional hearings (U.S.) 103–104
cultural studies 113–16, 119

D
diaspora studies 113–14
Divinity School (University of Chicago) 75, 77, 89, 119

E
Enlightenment 5–6, 49–50
essentialism(s) 1, 3–4, 14, 18, 80–81, 94–112
experience, religious 7, 50, 52, 54, 60–63, 65–66, 72–73, 77, 80–81, 86, 88, 93, 98–99, 112 see also faith

F
faith 2, 7, 50, 58, 60–63, 65, 68, 72–74, 81–85, 87–88, 96
Ford Foundation 35, 41, 43–44
Foreign Language and Area Studies (FLAS) Fellowship Program 40

G
Geist 14, 83
Geistwissenschaft 14
genealogy, genealogies 1, 4, 10, 26, 31–32, 52, 79, 86, 91, 93

H
Hamas 85
historical Jesus 74, 117
history 14–15, 90–91
    contrasted with faith 87–88
humanities 14, 94

I
identity politics 2, 6, 13, 24, 50–56, 70
imperialism see colonialism
Institute of Islamic Studies (McGill) 58–64, 67, 73–74, 94 see also Islam, graduate studies in
interdisciplinarity 49–51, 59, 114–15
intifada 101 see also Palestinian independence
introductory classes 79–81

Subject Index

introductory textbooks 67–70, 79–92
Iranian revolution 52, 101
Iraq 101, 109
Islam 25, 42–47
    Americanized Islam 3, 73–74
    attempts to undermine 13, 28–30, 77–78, 80–82
    "authentic" representations of 3–4, 54, 76–77, 80–81, 83–87, 93
    as "civilization" 4, 15, 56, 84
    contemporary representations 2, 11, 68–71, 107–8
    eternal truths of 93
    graduate studies in 74 *see also* Divinity School *and* Institute of Islamic Studies
    "hijacked" by extremists 55, 86–87, 93, 98, 110
    illegitimate expressions of 3, 84–85, 93–97
    monolithic 42, 45–46, 54, 69, 73–74, 80–84, 95–111
    reformation of 67–71
Islamic fundamentalism 91–92
Islamic studies 22, 24, 26, 32, 51, 59, 73–74, 92
    future prospects 10, 78, 92, 112–16
    invention of 4–5, 11–22, 33–34
    and religious studies 7–8, 42, 66, 72, 74–92, 99–111
Islamophobia 12, 29, 31
Israel 25, 39, 53, 69, 100–1
Ivory Towers on Sand 99–103

J

jihad 108
Jihad Watch 105
Judaism 2, 12, 16–18, 22–24, 81, 117

L

language 18–20, 25 *see also Volk*
Lebanon 52
Lewis–Said Exchange 9, 11–12, 29, 99, 102, 105

M

McGill University *see* Institute of Islamic Studies
media 2, 7, 54, 93–96
Middle East 56, 100–2
    conflicts in 12, 28–30, 104
    invention of 34–40, 47–48
Middle Eastern studies 1, 5, 12, 34–35, 41–48, 70, 73, 100–102, 118
Middle Eastern Studies Association (MESA) 103
Muslim Spain (al-Andalus) 15, 23

N

National Defense Foreign Language (NDFL) Fellowships 40
National Review 103
National Socialism 30–31
Near Eastern studies 1, 12, 70
neo-conservatives, neo-conservativism 11, 99
New Republic 103
New York Review of Books 9
New York Times 102, 104

O

oil 34
Oriental studies 11, 16, 37, 41–42, 48
Orientalism 2, 9, 11, 24–30, 38, 51–56, 73, 105–7
    British and French vs. German 5, 13, 26–27

P

Palestinian independence 5, 28
personal piety 65–66
philology 7, 65, 73, 90
    see also text/textuality
pre-Islamic Arabia 15, 22–23
Progressive Muslims 95, 109–11

Q

Qaeda, al- *see* al-Qaeda
Qur'ān 14, 16, 22–25, 27–28, 30, 68, 77–79, 82, 89–91, 109, 115

Quranic studies 16, 19–22, 27–28, 30–31, 77–79, 90–91, 115

R

religion
    assumptions of 3, 33–34, 54, 57, 61, 72–73, 75, 79–81, 87–89, 98, 113–14
    comparative 64, 92, 98–99
    essence of 34, 60–61, 87–89, 98
    models of 1, 3, 42–43, 59–60, 72–73, 98
    and violence 88–89, 108, 113–15
religious studies 5, 33–34, 100
    confusion with inter-faith dialogue 54, 59–60, 81, 88, 94, 109–11
    critical discourses within 2, 55–58, 70, 73, 78–80, 82–83, 92–93, 112–16
representation 53–56
Rockefeller Foundation 35, 41

S

sacred, irreducibility of 60
Second World War 6, 88
September 11, 2001 (9/11) 1–3, 11, 54–55, 87, 89, 93–112, 114
Shari'a 85–86, 89
Shoah 27
Social Science Research Council (SSRC) 38, 46
social sciences 27, 39–40, 94
"Steering Committee and Members, Section of the Study of Islam" 98
Sufism (Islamic mysticism) 31, 69
sui generis religion 33–35, 57–58, 66, 71–73, 75, 77 *see also* experience; religion

T

Taliban 69, 83, 88–89, 110
taxonomy, taxonomies *see* classification
terrorism 95, 97–98, 100, 108
    fight against 2, 101, 109
terrorist 3, 97
text/textuality 4, 73
    see also philology
Title VI 40–41, 102–3
tradition
    invention of 106
    rhetoric of 54–55, 105
Truth, regimes of 9, 54, 94

U

U.S. foreign policy 5, 37–40, 51–53, 102

V

Verstehen ("understanding") 6, 73, 91–92
Volk 14, 18

W

Wahhabi, Wahhabism *see* Islamic fundamentalism
Washington 35, 101–2
Washington Post 102
Weimar Germany 5, 12
Wissenschaft 14–15
Wissenschaft des Judentums 15–18
world religions 46

Y

Yom Kippur War 28–29 *see also* Middle East, conflicts in

Z

Zionism 9, 28, 101

Index of Names

Adams, Charles 74–79, 100, 119
Ahmad, Aijaz 53
Anidjar, Gil 5, 12
Armstrong, Karen 7, 55, 87–89
Arnal, William E. 56
Asad, Talal 24
Atta, Muhammad 97
Avicenna (ibn Sina) 66
Ayoub, Mahmoud 81–83, 94

Berg, Herbert 24, 28
Bin Laden, Osama 86, 108
Binder, Leonard 33
Brauer, Jerald C. 75
Brockelmann, Carl 26

Cantwell Smith, Wilfred see Smith, Wilfred Cantwell
Cohen, Mark R. 15
Conant, James B. 37–38
Conrad, Lawrence I. 11, 16, 27
Cook, Michael 1, 28, 120
Cracknell, Kenneth 59
Crone, Patricia 1, 28

Daniel, Norman 20
Denny, Frederick M. 67, 89–92
Dickens, Charles 112
Dubuisson, Daniel 34, 36, 95
Duchesne-Guillemin, Jacques 43–44
Durkheim, Emil 35–37
Dylan, Bob 94

Eliade, Mircea 60, 65–66, 76, 118
Esposito, John L. 7, 55, 81, 84–87, 105, 108–9, 120

Falwell, Jerry 119
Ferahian, Salwa 58
Firestone, Reuven 31
Fitzgerald, Timothy 43, 86, 88

Foucault, Michel 24, 52
Freytag, Georg Wilhelm 17
Fück, Johann 30

Geertz, Clifford 55
Geiger, Abraham 5, 9, 12–24, 25, 29–30, 104, 115, 117
Geiger, Ludwig 17, 31
Gibb, Hamilton Alexander Rosskeen 46–47
Gold, Daniel 15
Goldziher, Ignaz 16, 26–27, 29, 76
Graham, William 117
von Grunebaum, Gustav 43–44

Hall, Robert B. 37–38
Hegel, Georg Wilhelm Friedrich 14
Hentsch, Thierry 20, 34, 113, 117
Herder, Johann Gottfried 18
Heschel, Susannah 17, 117
Hirschfeld, Hartwig 30
Hobsbawm, Eric J. 106
Hodgson, Marshal G.S. 7, 50, 64–66, 82, 107, 119
Horovitz, Joseph 16, 29–31
Hughes, Aaron W. 10–11, 15, 23, 73–74, 78–79, 106, 115, 117, 119
von Humboldt, Wilhelm 18
Hussein, Saddam 110

ibn Gabirol 23

James, William 72, 78
Juschka, Darlene M. 50

Kant, Immanuel 86
Kippenberg, Hans G. 18
Kitigawa, Joseph M. 118
Koltun-Fromm, Ken 17
Kramer, Martin 7, 11, 30, 41, 99–105, 118, 120

Kraus, Paul 16
Kugel, James L. 31
Kurtz, Stanley 103

Laroui, Abdallah 24
Lassner, Jacob 17, 21, 31
Levine, Mark 55
Lewis, Bernard 9, 11, 16, 29, 45–46, 99, 105, 118
Lincoln, Bruce 18, 36, 55–57, 72, 74, 82, 88, 92, 97–99, 106
Lockman, Zachary 5, 11, 40, 46–47, 103
Lopez Jr., Donald S. 33

Mack, Michael 14–15
Maimonides, Moses 23
Martin, Richard C. 67
Masuzawa, Tomoko 4, 16, 33, 113
Mauss, Marcel 35–37
McCutcheon, Russell T. 11, 43, 55, 57, 75, 79, 86, 97, 118, 120
Mendes-Flohr, Paul 15
Moosa, Ebrahim 70–71, 119
Muhammad 9, 19, 21–23
Müller, F. Max 98–99
Myers, David N. 15, 17

Nasr, Seyyed Hossein 7, 55, 105–108
Newby, Gordon D. 117
Nietzsche, Friedrich Wilhelm 9–10, 12
Nöldeke, Theodor 22, 26
Novick, Peter 14

Orsi, Robert A. 3, 33, 55, 87–88, 114
Owen, Roger 24, 34

Pearlmann, Moshe 22
Pipes, Daniel 104
Preus, J. Samuel 73, 75
Proudfoot, Wayne 86, 106
Pusey, Nathan M. 83

Qutb, Sayyid 92

Rahman, Fazlur 7, 50, 66–70, 91, 119
von Ranke, Leopold 14
Renan, Ernst 16, 27, 29
Rippin, Andrew 24, 120
Rodinson, Maxime 27, 113

de Sacy, Antoine-Isaac Silvestre 16, 21, 27, 29
Safi, Omid 70, 109–10, 120
Said, Edward W. 5, 9, 11, 13, 16, 24–29, 31, 51–52, 81, 99, 101, 105
Schaeder, Hans Heinrich 30
Schapiro, Israel 30
Scharf, Robert 86, 106
Schelling, Friedrich Wilhelm Joseph 14
Schleiermacher, Friedrich 86, 106–7
Schorsch, Ismar 15, 17
Sells, Michael A. 91, 117
Shaw, Rosalind 50
Slater, Robert 59
Smith, Jonathan Z. 4, 32, 49
Smith, Wilfred Cantwell 7, 50, 58–64, 67–68, 76, 80, 97–98, 107, 118
Speyer, Heinrich 16, 30
Stetkevych, Jaroslav 77–78
Steward, Julian H. 39
Strenski, Ivan 118
Szanton, David L. 118

Turner, Bryan S. 65–66, 119

Wallerstein, Immanuel 42
Walzer, Richard 66
Wansbrough, John 28
Wasserstrom, Steven M. 88
Waugh, Earle H. 67
Weil, Gotthold 16
Weil, Gustav 16, 27
White, Hayden 14
Wiebe, Donald 80
Wiener, Max 17
Wolfson, Harry Austryn 16

Young, F.M. 117